Visiting Martin Amis

Visiting Martin Amis

JULIA CLINCH

ISBN-13: **9781542408721**
ISBN-10: **1542408725**
Library of Congress Control Number: 2017900366
CreateSpace Independent Publishing Platform
North Charleston, South Carolina

For: Elaine Cole Cornell
Sara and Jeff Roberts
Vicki G. Rambin

• • •

Table of Contents

Introduction

The title, *Visiting Martin Amis,* reflects Amis's non-fiction collection, *Visiting Mrs. Nabokov* (1993). It's a memoir of the author that *Commentary* magazine has called "the most famous living British writer" (October 2012). It's as memory serves it, my experience with Martin Amis over the years—a personal view that shines light on the man as well as the writer.

> Martin Louis Amis (born 25 August 1949) second son to British novelist, Sir Kingsley Amis, is a first-rate novelist in his own right, with *Money* (1984) and *London Fields* (1989). Martin Amis received the James Tait Black Memorial Prize for a memoir, *Experience,* and has been listed for the Booker Prize in 1991 for his novel, *Time's Arrow* and in 2003 for *Yellow Dog.* Amis served as the Professor of Creative Writing at the Centre for New Writing at the University of Manchester. In 2008, *London Times* named him one of the fifty greatest British writers since 1945.
>
> —Amazon.com/books [1]

---

1 https://www.amazon.com/Martin-Amis/e/B000APW594/ref=sr_tc_2_0?qid=1505721997&sr=1-2-ent

I met first Martin Amis in 1987 when he agreed to an interview I had requested in a letter in care of his London publisher, Jonathan Cape, Inc. After we made arrangements on the phone, I flew to London from Los Angeles to interview Amis twice in his West London writing studio. The books, films, politics, and pop culture we discussed at the time may be unfamiliar to younger readers; but fans that have followed Amis's career will know the terrain well. This is an insight to Martin Amis off guard, before and during his midlife changes.

After I returned to Los Angeles, Martin and I developed a friendship via transatlantic telephone calls and written correspondence, as well as rendezvous on his American book tours. In L.A., we had dinner at the Beverly Wilshire and Sofitel Hotel in Beverly Hills. Martin sent me the proof of *Time's Arrow*, his novel about the Holocaust before it was published in 1991.

From the 1980s, Martin Amis has amassed a huge following of loyal readers and fans around the world. He relished and recorded the bizarre, turbulent atmosphere of Britain and the US during the 1970s and 80s, arguably the transformative period of the late 20th century. "No other contemporary writer has proved so magnetic for the popular press: he has, despite himself, achieved celebrity status. Of late, his reputation as a novelist has been matched by his outspoken, challenging writing on contemporary global politics, and he has earned the status as 'the Orwell of the early twenty-first century.'" — Amazon Books

This memoir also describes living in Hollywood during the hedonistic 1970s and '80s when I was a young actress. (My TV credits include *Starsky & Hutch, Hart to Hart, The Rockford Files,* and an ABC sit-com series.) It was an era of excess, extravagance, "unsafe" sex, crescendos of cocaine, and the greatest rock-and-roll bands ever recorded—topics and themes Amis featured in his novels during the same period. My close friends included Pamela G., who was once under contract with Twentieth-Century Fox studios at the same time as Marilyn Monroe and cousin to the head of the Manhattan Project; and actress Phyllis Davis who dated and lived with Dean Martin (I often joined them at Dean's favorite Italian restaurants.)

I knew Hollywood celebrities: Warren Beatty, (the late) James Garner and Richard Pryor who were charming; others were not. I encountered Jack Nicholson, Peter Lawford, Ed Ruscha; and British authors: Julian Barnes, Ian McEwan; and (the late) Christopher Hitchens.

Documentation is from correspondence (handwritten or typed by Martin) over the years. This memoir is not authorized; therefore, Amis's 13 letters remain private and unpublished. Martin sent me a photo of himself at twenty-five in Paris (on the cover). The two interviews with Amis were transcribed from cassette tapes recorded with his consent in his West London flat. Parts of Amis's letters are discreetly summarized for contextual continuity.

Martin Amis has written fourteen novels and continues to write in his late sixties. His popular novels include *The Rachel Papers, Money, London Fields, The Information, and Time's Arrow*. His memoir, *Experience* (2000) was critically acclaimed. To date, *The Rachel Papers, Dead Babies,* and *London Fields* have been produced into films. His last novel, *The Zone of Interest* (2014) is set in Auschwitz during WWII.

A keen interest in politics spurred Amis to write *Koba, the Dread: Laughter and the Twenty Million,* a gripping portrait of the evils of Joseph Stalin. *The Second Plane: September 11* story on terrorist Muhammad Atta, leader of Islamist hijackers that toppled the Twin Towers.

Amis's fiction includes *Einstein's Monsters* and *Heavy Water and Other Stories;* his journalism and essays are in *The Moronic Inferno, Visiting Mrs. Nabokov,* and *The War Against Cliché;* his latest, *The Rub of Time: Bellow,*

Julia Clinch

Nabokov, Hitchens, Travolta, Trump: Essays and Reportage, 1986-2016. [2] Amis
often expresses his views on American politics. He is a liberal.

• • •

---

2 Martin Amis, *The Rub of Time: Bellow, Nabokov, Hitchens, Travolta, Trump: Essays and Reportage,* 1986-2016. New York, Alfred A. Knopf, Feb. 2018

One

The Event Horizon

I had just returned from a weekend in Rosarito Beach, Mexico, when I saw a letter with British stamps and a London return address in my mailbox. Climbing the stairs to my Beverly Hills courtyard apartment, I opened the envelope to find a typed message from Martin Amis with a phone number to call in London for an interview I had requested; he'd added, 'the photograph helped.'

Whoa. The British author I'd written over a month ago had actually responded to my letter, and even more, he had given me a phone number and asked me to call him! Now I could arrange an interview with him next month, time enough to plan a trip to England. Frankly I was amazed that Martin Amis, a famous author in Britain, would reply to a letter from someone he'd never met or heard of. I smiled to myself when I read that the photograph helped.

The photo I had enclosed in the letter was of me standing in front of gray stone stairs in a garden in Holmby Hills, an exclusive area in Beverly Hills where celebrities and the wealthy live, including the late Hugh Hefner in his Playboy Mansion. (At the time I was on the guest list for the Mansion's Friday movie night that Hef and his "Manly Night" inner circle of friends had selected to view after a sumptuous dinner buffet.) While posing, I saw Richard Gere carrying a tennis racket on his way to a private court. I wore a formfitting top and short skirt just above the knees. It was conservative by Hollywood standards, but provocative by others'.

Photo sent to Martin

• • •

At the time, I was dating Greg, a young artist who worked for L.A.'s famous modern artist, Ed Ruscha. We had driven down to Rosarito Beach in Baja California, the long Mexican peninsula lying in the Pacific Ocean. The summer before the trip I had read Martin's short story,

"Insight at Flame Lake," in *Vanity Fair.* [3] The story had made such a deep impression on me that I felt compelled to write the author in London. I'd never heard of Martin Amis, but his fictional story spoke to me on a subconscious level. I had underlined the words: *"I have a reality problem. Oh yeah? Reality has the reality problem. Reality is right out of control and could try anything at any time."* Meanwhile, my own conscious plane was in perennial Kierkegäardian angst. Nonetheless—existentially, I was fairly good at appearing under control.

My original letter:

To: Martin Amis
Jonathan Cape Ltd, Inc.
Kensington Gardens Square
London W-2, England

McCarty Drive
Beverly Hills, California 90212
August 12, 1987
Dear Mr. Amis,

Having read *The Moronic Inferno, Einstein's Monsters,* and *Money* and looking forward to *Success,* I am convinced you are a writer with a very bright future.

I will be in London in November, and have queried *Esquire* who gave me a positive response by calling me directly in July about several topics I wish to research while in England, including you. Would you be kind enough to let me know if it is possible to contact you while in London and set up an interview?

---

3 Martin Amis, "Insight at Flame Lake." *Vanity Fair,* June 1987, p. 98-126+.

Enclosed is my photo and theatrical résumé so that you have some information on me. I teach literature in Beverly Hills part-time. I hope the fact that I have been an actress is not held against me.

Looking forward to hearing from you at your earliest convenience.

Truly yours,
Julienne Wells

P.S. Your short story "Insight at Flame Lake" in *Vanity Fair* is nothing less than brilliant.

• • •

For the record, there is no letter to *Esquire*; hence, no response. In truth I was an actress and schoolteacher. In 1987, I was prone to exaggerate (Okay, embellish…but then I did live in Hollywood). A good friend called it chutzpah. Not expecting to hear back from the British author, I forgot all about my letter.

Now that Martin Amis contacted me, I dove into a flurry of research on him at the Beverly Hills Library. With no Internet or Google in 1987, I ferreted out information about Amis on the library's prototype computer that printed out titles of his novels, book reviews, and essays from rolls of paper with perforated edges. Older articles were photocopied on microfilm in archives that had to be rolled by hand on the library's reel-to-reel apparatus.

I discovered Martin Amis, age 38, was famous in Great Britain after his first novel, *The Rachel Papers*, was published when he was only twenty-four. Three more dark, comedic novels soon followed the popular best seller. Son of renowned author, Kingsley Amis (knighted Sir Kingsley), Martin Amis had already chiseled out a successful writing career for himself and was labeled a "Young Turk" and called "The Mick Jagger of Letters" (also, "a little shit," in literary circles). Photographs of the young author revealed he was strikingly good looking with an aura of sensual *savoir-faire*. In all the magazine and newspaper pictures, Martin Amis appeared to be the proverbial tall, dark, and handsome. More so, he exuded an air of come-hither. Martin Amis looked like a bad boy—just my type.

• • •

Thrilled at getting a response to my unsolicited letter, I immediately replied to the English author—this time personally addressing the envelope to his London flat:

To: Martin Amis
Leamington Road Villas
London W-11, England

Dear Martin Amis,

Your letter was waiting in my mailbox when I returned from a trip to Mexico last week. It made my day. Thank you for your note and phone number. My trip to London is still in the works, thank goodness, since I just now heard from you.

I substituted as head of the Theater Arts Dept. today, hence, the stationery. I teach English, as I mentioned, but wish to expedite my writing, and that is why I called you to schedule our appointment this morning. I reached a woman who told me you'd be back Monday, but I didn't leave my number.

This week I did some research on you in the Beverly Hills Library: book reviews, interviews, magazine articles and features. I did not find one negative review of any of your novels in this country. Amazing, since our critics love to excoriate a novel as much as I imagine yours do. I'm glad they have the sense to know a good author when they read one, and then to encourage him with a good review.

But what an *enfant terrible* they make you out to be, e.g., *Esquire*, January 1987, by A. Smith. This hearsay doesn't faze me, as I've always preferred good looking 'bad boys,' a peccadillo of mine, I have to admit.

Hope we can find a mutual time schedule to meet. Looking forward to it, to say the least.

Yours truly,
Julienne Wells

• • •

The following week, Martin and I spoke on the phone. He said to let him know when I was in London and he'd find time for an interview.

Meanwhile, I did more research on Martin at the library, photocopying articles and reviews on his books, journalism, and many photographs. By this time, I'd gathered a lot of information and was eager to meet him in London as we had planned on the phone. He was married with two young sons. Oh well, I wasn't going to sleep with him. After all, I already had a boyfriend and had no intention of doing that. Nevertheless, being a healthy woman who liked handsome men, I knew I'd push the envelope as far as I could without turning my moral compass sideways. Having fun flirting wasn't against the law, was it?

I quickly got a good deal with British Airlines: a round-trip ticket from Los Angeles to London that included a week at an older, but pleasant hotel with a full, English breakfast in Bloomsbury Square—around the corner from the British Museum— all for $450.00. My goal was to meet and interview bad boy, Martin Amis, as soon as possible.

• • •

Two

Insight in London Fields

"We just stand at the jaws of the cave, and strike a match, and quickly ask if anybody there."

– Martin Amis, *Money: A Suicide Note* [4]

The last week of November 1987, I flew to London, checked into my hotel, and immediately called Martin. He said he would be busy until the following Monday but to call then, and he would tell me what time to meet him at his writing flat. Afterward I called my cousin, Owen, who lived in London's posh section of Notting Hill with his wife and two sons to tell him I was in London and hoped to visit. Owen sounded glad I was in town and invited me to have dinner with them. Meanwhile, I had the weekend to explore London and see its spectacular sights. I started with the British Museum, a short walking distance from my Bloomsbury hotel. Admission is free to the public—a gift of her majesty, the Queen, to her royal subjects.

I climbed the multiple stairs of the enormous entrance to the museum's granite floor lobby, and walked over the intricate, tessera mosaics

---

4 Martin Amis. *Money: A Suicide Note,* London: Jonathan Cape, Ltd., 1st Edition. 1984.

imported from the excavated villas of Rome's wealthy citizens. (Tesserae are small, individually colored, cube shaped tiles used to create elaborate mosaic pictures on villa floors.) I began my tour of the huge halls filled with invaluable antiquities that displayed the classical art and culture of ancient Greece, and of the Roman Empire that flourished in three hundred years of the prosperous *Pax Romana*. I was captivated by the unending, gigantic rooms of art which illustrated thousands of years of Western civilization; e.g., BC Greek statues; hundreds of busts and eroded sculptures of Roman patricians, equestrian generals; and the famous Elgin Marbles—the twenty-five hundred years old Parthenon reliefs—known for Lord Elgin, who brought them to England. To peruse the Rosetta Stone alone is worth the flight to London.

I walked around by myself, eavesdropping on various tour guides and groups. Ceiling-high Egyptian obelisks, encased Pharaoh mummies embedded with gems, and Hittite chariots were on view in the ancient Egyptian area. The five thousand-year old sarcophaguses and mummies fascinated me, as did the Pharaohs' arcane tomb items buried with them that have survived from Egypt's ancient empires. Assyrian and Babylonian reliefs carved out from their original ancient walls by British archeologists and crews loomed over the halls.

I asked a guide if the word "Assyrian," used to describe some reliefs, was reflected in the modern nation of Syria. Her face curled up curiously and she said she wasn't sure. It had to be.

Eager to explore, I climbed staircases to more ancient monuments. British archaeologists had filled thousands of foreign treasures in cargo ships to bring to Queen Victoria, which she shared with her royal subjects, the British people. Now the despoliations, loot, and fortune delighted me immeasurably. The Queen named one of the four Pekingese dogs, "Looty" that Captain Cook brought her from the Forbidden City in Peking, China. The British conquerors took full advantage of the manifest *Victori spolia* (to the victor go the spoils) in their victorious campaigns. HRM Queen Victoria was eponymous with the extraordinary conquests of the British Empire in the Victorian Age of the 19th Century.

I spent several hours exploring the magnificent treasure trove in the mammoth museum and still did not see all its treasure. That evening after walking all day, I wanted to get off my feet, so I took the Tube to the theater district to see Agatha Christie's mystery play *Ten Little Indians*, which had been showing for several decades. (Christie's original title was *Ten Little N——s.*)

On Sunday morning after a good night's sleep, I indulged in the hotel's English breakfast, which consisted of scrambled eggs, sausage, thick ham, bacon, poached eggs, toast, crumpets, orange marmalade, red currant jelly and strawberry jam, butter, pancakes and maple syrup (it was like a Las Vegas buffet). Then walked or took the Underground—the Tube—all over London from morning until late at night, surfeiting my eyes, ears, and nose with the fascinating sights, sounds, and smells of London. I sensed what nineteenth-century writer James Boswell felt when he arrived in this magnificent city in 1762, and like Boswell, I fell in love with Londontown.

London visit

Late Monday morning, I called Martin. He told me to come to his flat in Notting Hill at 4:00 p.m. when he usually finished writing for the day. Eager to make a good impression, I wanted to look my best. After showering I sprayed Chanel Number 5 over my shoulder-length hair and carefully applied my makeup. I chose a black, form-fitting, wool skirt I'd bought on Rodeo Drive that had slits on the sides, showing a hint of my lower thigh when I walked, and a peacock-teal, cashmere turtleneck. Because London was chilly, verging on cold, I wore a mink waist-jacket, and then stepped into pointy, black suede pumps pointed in his direction.

Hailing a London taxi (it's like a huge, black SUV) I told the cabby to drive to Leamington Road Villas. Arriving at the corner I paid the driver and walked down the narrow street until I saw Martin's address on an old, two-story Victorian duplex at the end corner. (Martin later told me it had once been a church rectory.)

Entering the small, brick courtyard, I went up to the door and saw the name AMIS scrawled under a buzzer and pushed it. Waiting anxiously at the threshold, I expected a tall, dark, and handsome man whom I'd seen in the magazine photos to appear. Instead, the door opened to reveal a short, pallid man with a large forehead and saffron wisps of hair flying about his head, standing in front of me. My instant glance didn't get to the generous Mick-lips. I stood transfixed at what appeared like an alien that had just stepped out of a UFO. (Martin told later me I had winced.) Shaken by the reality of his appearance in person, I followed outer-space man up the narrow, winding staircase to his flat on the second floor, quite literally in shock.

Martin led me into a little kitchen and asked me if I'd like a cup of coffee. At this point, I would have liked a shot of whiskey. He got out a small metal pot, put in grounds and water, and brewed coffee over a small stove. (Later I told him I thought it was instant coffee, but he assured me that it had been brewed.) Still dazed, I didn't know what was happening, or why I was alone with E.T. All I knew for sure was that this person did not look remotely like the photos I'd seen in the Beverly Hills Library of the author Martin Amis.

Visiting Martin Amis

Martin's voice is smooth and seductive (but not pretentious): as it were, Oxfordian, and he takes full advantage of this, having seduced women with it ever since his days at Oxford University. Martin later told me he knew he "had me in his hand within five minutes." He was correct, although I wanted to see how this literary adventure (by Gothic standards) would play out. After all, I'd flown across the North American continent and Atlantic Ocean to meet and interview this British author. Therefore, I quickly adjusted to the strange reality before me: a different-looking man than I had expected, but with the charm of an enchanter.

Taking our coffee into the living room, we began with the usual icebreakers, "How was your trip, Julie? Did you have a good flight?" Martin mentioned that he had had a girlfriend by the name of Julie when he was younger. I told him I had seen he had dedicated the novel, *Dead Babies,* to her. Also, he said that Wells was the surname of another girlfriend he'd had.

As I lay out pages of the Xeroxed periodicals and clippings I'd brought with me on the coffee table, we began to talk about his writing. Martin told me he was working on a new novel, titled *London Fields,* and led me into a small side room where the biggest, old typewriter I'd ever seen was sitting on a narrow counter over a straight back chair. It was hard to believe the little counter could hold up the huge, clunky machine. Martin chuckled and agreed it was "a heapy, old thing." I saw a sheet of white paper with typing in the roller of the heapy, old thing that Martin was working on for the final draft of the novel.

Martin reached up to the shelf above the typewriter for three of his books, *Success, Money,* and *Einstein's Monsters,* and handed them to me. I had just purchased *Einstein's Monsters* at Whitestone bookstore that weekend and gave it back. I thanked him for the two books and we returned to the living room to discuss his current novel.

Martin sat down in a chair diagonally from me on the sofa. After Martin gave me permission to record the interview, I set the mini-recorder on the coffee table and pressed Record.

The setting of his new novel took place in London, but the title, *London Fields,* had actually come to him while riding the train when he worked for *The New Statesman,* after he had graduated from Oxford. As the train passed through the suburbs, he watched the empty fields outside the passenger window—appropriately called London Fields— that mysteriously appealed to him. The plot involved a murder mystery, except that this crime would be about a "murderee," a woman who had come to London to find her murderer. Her name was Nicola Six. Martin explained the theory that some people are born predisposed to be murdered; they have a peculiar DNA that attracts them to a murderer. And Nicola Six had this gene.

Martin had chosen the female protagonist's name, Nicola Six, as a double entendre of six and sex. The villain was the nefarious Keith Talent—adding he thought the name 'Keith' was especially hideous. For some reason, it struck Martin as repulsive. He said his friends, aware of his aversion to the name, called him "Little Keith."

For amusement, Martin began talking about people's weird names— laughing at the sexual innuendos and funny ones.

"In America, there are all sorts of strange names—I knew someone named Susie Clapp. There's an American surname of Orifice. Can you imagine Julie Orifice?"

I chimed in, "My surname is really Clinch—so I'm Julie Clinch. I used Wells, my Screen Actors Guild name, in my letters to you."

Martin's face lit up, and he asked, "How do you spell it?"

"C-L-I-N-C-H," I replied.

"That...*Clinch*...is the name of the protagonist in my novel."

We both sat silent for a moment, processing the uncanny coincidence. An eerie sensation came over me, and I fell backward on the sofa.

Looking up, I whined, "Reality is for people who can't handle drugs. This is reality I can't handle."

• • •

Three

MARTIN AMIS: OFF GUARD: PART 1

In the following interview with Martin Amis in his London writing studio, he talked about his new novel, *London Fields*. His literary paragon, Saul Bellow called Amis, already a best-selling author in England, "A Joyce or Flaubert, with signs of genius."

While the novel was still in the final draft on his typewriter, Amis philosophized about the characters, good and evil, in the narrative. A literary moralist, Amis revealed how closely he identified with his protagonist, a young American writer who strategically migrates to trendy West London—a writer who finds writing a novel morally wrong because "you invent these people" and "then you punish them like a God would." Amis explained how he "gets around this uneasiness and turns postmodernism on its head."

His cool demeanor aside, Amis touched on everything from *King Lear* to morality to the delights of indulgence. The following pages were transcribed from two recorded interviews with the author.

Interview: Part One – London: Dec. 1987

"Nice guys are no fun to read about."

— MARTIN AMIS

Martin Amis [MA]: The name of my new novel is *London Fields*. It's just outside London, and when I worked for *The New Statesman*, I had to go to the printer, and the train went through there. I thought it was such a vague, pathetic, and beautiful name for something to be called. But, of course, it isn't fields anymore; it's factories. Anyway, it stuck in my mind, and then I just thought it'll be right for the novel because of the 'fields' idea; there are these three characters that have, as it were, "fields of attraction and repulsion."

J. Clinch [JC]: Gravitational fields?

MA: Yes, and the central idea of the book, where the catalyst that gets things going is—this may not be so in nature —but the girl character is what is called "a murderee." Do you understand that?

JC: Yes, she's going to be murdered. She's the victim of the murderer.

MA: She's the sort of person who, all her life this was going to happen to her.

JC: Her destiny?

MA: That's right. There's this theory that some people who are murdered are destined thus; there's something about them that makes them become murdered…a chemical.

JC: Hmmm…That's an interesting concept.

MA: And she has to sort of arrange it, in a way.

JC: She knows it.

MA: Yes, and she accepted it, and she, in fact, encourages it.

JC: Brings it about via the *Looking for Mr. Goodbar* thing?

MA: Right.

JC: Not consciously, but she's asking for it.

MA: Yes, she's asking for it, and it has to happen on a certain night. But in fact, although it's a murder story of a kind, it's the wrong way around. It's not so much of a "who done it" but a "who will do it?"

JC: Yes, is she trying to control this?

MA: Yes, absolutely, completely control it; synchronize it.

JC: I mean things we're insecure about, things we can't control and are so at odds with—like the fact we have to die. It gives us some kind of power when we do control it; hence, suicide, mastery over life and death kind of thing.

MA: Yeah. In fact, it's sort of, in a way it can be seen as a proxy suicide, a surrogate suicide.

JC: Well, sure it is.

MA: Except you get someone else to do it for you. Then you go out in a blaze of glory.

JC: Two to tango, so to speak.

MA: That's right, you're not complete without the other.

JC: Which is the good and the evil thing.

MA: Well, it just strikes me as a true thing about babies, they're both heaven and hell.

JC: At the same time, in the same baby.

MA: It's a true thing about them. They're also, paradoxically, an ordinary miracle. The most extraordinary thing in the world is to produce a child; but, also axiomatically, the most banal thing.

JC: Because animals can do it,

MA: It's the first thing a gay man does, a gay woman does.

(Note: I'm not gay, but I disagree that it's not the first thing a gay woman does. Gay women, as a rule, behave sexually differently than gay men—as do their counterparts.)

JC: It's the most banal, at the same time, the most majestic and divine, and it's still the good and evil thing being enmeshed.

MA: That's right, and that's what appeals to me in this book: the good child is the daughter of the villain, and the bad child is the son of the good character. It's the first time I've tried to make—do it seriously—a good character. It's very hard to do.

JC: Why is it that nice boys are boring? Bad boys are so much more exciting...sexy. But I think drugs and alcohol are a form of evil.

MA: The myth has been stated many times, the Jekyll and Hyde, a classic metaphor for drink. You have a drink and the id takes over, instead of the ego and you go to whores and beat beggars on the streets.

JC: I like where John Self in your novel *Money* went to a hooker, but he could not bring himself to have sex with her when he found out she was pregnant. Again, you bring in a baby—that hallowed ground that he could not trespass.

MA: That's right, except that it occurs to him while he lectures her, what the hell, he might as well get a hand job of it.

JC: Yeah, that's not so bad. It's not invading the sanctified baby, per se. A hand job is external. I can see how if he'd been drinking, he could rationalize that. Anyway, back to *London Fields*, are there three or four characters?

MA: It's complicated because there's this fourth person. You're familiar with the post-modernist, which means the writer will keep reminding his reader that this is a novel. I want to turn that on its head. That is what I'm doing because my character is American who comes to London in the year 1999.

JC: Oh, futuristic?

MA: Just a little, the millennium. His thing is that he wants to try and write something, although he's got a reputation as a journalist and a travel writer and so on, but he can't write a novel. There are all sorts of complicated reasons why he can't write a novel. He can't make anything up. He finds it morally uneasy...making things up.

JC: He finds it dishonest?

MA: Yeah, there's conventions about the novel he doesn't like. Anyway, he's never been able to do it.

JC: It's beneath him in some way?

MA: No, it's more the thing that always worried me, that you create characters and then you punish them. What does all that mean?

JC: But we do that in real life—create popular heroes, and then we desecrate them, like Marilyn Monroe, and John Kennedy, and Lady Diana. At least, until they unexpectedly die; then we glorify and lionize them as like saints.

Visiting Martin Amis

(Note: Lady Diana Spencer was alive at this time. When she tragically died ten years later in a car accident, she became the martyred People's Princess).

MA: Sure, but that's sort of a mass thing, a real human urge. What worries his protagonist is that when you write a novel, you're in a god-like position. You assign life to all, and then you destroy it and ruin it. Anyway, what happens, he arrives in London in a very sinister way; he sees these events going on—sees these three people. With a strange subtlety, he gets to know all three of them, and he infiltrates their houses and so on. He deliberately sets out to get to know them because he can see this drama built into them. So he can't write a novel, but he can write this true story.

JC: Yes! So he's not being apocryphal.

MA: Yes, and he's reminding the reader that it's really happening. It's not literature—it's true life.

JC: The fiction non-fiction novel, Capote did that.

MA: Yeah, except that mine *isn't* real— it's made up by me!

JC: I'm going to devil's advocate this because if you're going to make up a character—why would you call him John Self in *Money*? I mean, come on, Martin.

MA: I think it's a great name.

JC: It's also "my self."

MA: Yeah, it is "my-self," but there is someone called John Self. It's a perfect name because John is the most common Christian name.

JC: Also, Self is an alter ego of yours. I heard someone accused you of putting a character in *Money* named Martin Amis to throw the reader off— that John Self wasn't you, and you denied it.

MA: I partially denied it. I mean it crossed my mind. I wouldn't want people to think I was like John Self.

JC: You dismissed it. But I think you must have been involved with some of the—these people to produce such an accurate novel about the film world. By the way, has anyone bought the film rights to *Money*?

MA: Yes, it's optioned.

JC: I think it'd make a great movie.

MA: I think it'll be good. The guy who's directing it is coming over soon, Adam Brooks.

JC: Again, in *London Fields*, like in the film, *The Onion Fields*—a lot of things happened in fields.

MA: Yes, I like James Woods. He starred in that.

JC: I do too, but it was a depressing story. Is your novel going to be depressing?

MA: I don't think so.

JC: Life is depressing enough without reading about it.

MA: That's a funny argument that's put to rest all the time if it's a good story.

JC: If it's worth it— like you said —if the story is good enough the author can get away with anything.

MA: I mean that subject matter, even if it deals with the most dismal kind doesn't condition your response to it. You can come out of *King Lear* feeling exalted, in fact.

JC: I agree.

MA: When I read it, I'm just grateful there is such literature. The events, after all, I made out to make different kinds of points. Shakespeare is saying life can be awful and unjust…

JC: And, what about redemption, life can be redeemable.

MA: The book is the redemption, the writing.

JC: Whose writing?

MA: Shakespeare, in this case.

JC: Sure, but is your writing the redemption in *London Fields?*

MA: Yeah, it's everything that gives pleasure that a novel is shaped for.

JC: The sweet and sour, the good and evil?

MA: Yeah, some hysterical girl at a lecture I gave in Denmark turned on me for being gloomy, and she said, "Come on, man, I mean, there's really some neat people in this world, why don't you write about them?"

JC: I think she was trying to make her own statement.

MA: Trying to be positive and 'upbeat.'

JC: I told a girl I met going to the National Opera that I didn't go to musicals often because of the continuous tap-dancing. The non-stop happiness gets a bit banal. I need conflict, something dramatic to get my teeth into. People who are always this wonderful Pollyanna. Let's face it, they're too saccharine.

MA: Yeah.

(At that outburst, I wondered what Martin was thinking of my going out on a limb with his 'upbeat' comment, adding my two cents. So impulsive, *moi.*)

JC: Women in America have literally gotten away with killing their own child using the defense of postpartum depression syndrome. What do you think of that?

MA: John Self says that that premenstrual tension is enough of a hazard without judges letting girls off for stabbing their boyfriends.

JC: (laughing) I know. Did you hear about the Twinkies defense?

MA: What are Twinkies?

JC: A little cake sold in convenience stores.

MA: (thinking) ... Glucose...the Twinkies defense.

JC: (laughing at his hard line delivery) Mayor Moscone was killed, remember, in San Francisco? That guy went in and shot two people in the mayor's office. Dan White used the Twinkies defense in his trial, claiming chemicals in junk food made him unbalanced and caused him to kill Moscone and Milk.

MA: He wasn't Harvey Milk?

JC: Yes, Milk was the homosexual who got killed. And the guy who killed him got off because it was rumored that killing a homosexual wasn't as bad as killing a hetero. He was convicted of manslaughter and served about five years in prison before being released in 1984. Anyway, the murderer ended up killing himself. (I pointed my finger to my head and pulled an imaginary trigger.) No one gave him any peace after that.

MA: Oh, really?

JC: Yeah.

MA: The Twinkies defense. I'll remember that. If I ever do anything wicked, I'll plead that.

JC: But you have to get something more germane to England, like Mars candy bars. In any case, truth is stranger than fiction.

MA: It certainly is. The West Coast is.

JC: Well, we have Greyhound therapy.

MA: The Greyhound dog?

JC: It's the name of our bus lines. Now that Reagan has let everyone out of the insane asylums.

MA: I know—they're all wandering around the streets.

JC: Yeah, and back East they didn't want them wandering around the streets in New York, Detroit, Philadelphia, or Baltimore, so they gave them a one way ticket to L.A.—on the Greyhound bus. That's why they call it Greyhound therapy.

MA: Jesus! Who let them get away with that?

JC: It's just one of those things where no one stopped it. Like the little trick Castro played on president Carter. He sent AIDS along with Cuba's undesirables to America as well as many Haitians *personas non-gratis*.

MA: Emptied the prisons.

JC: Hey, did he get the last laugh?

MA: Yeah.

JC: So what did you tell this woman who wants you to write about jovial people?

MA: I sort of beat her up a bit. This is another point. The very medium of stories tends toward awfulness of one kind or another because if you have a hard time—or your friend's letter that comes telling of pleasant meals and of good weather and comfortable hotels— isn't as much fun to read as the one that tells of missed flights, lost passports, etc.

JC: You mean to the people this happens to. It's schadenfreude, a perverse joy you get from another's misfortune.

MA: If you've had a disastrous holiday, the letter will be better than if you haven't.

JC: Oh. Unless you can't write the letter because you're dead.

MA: Well, drawing it short of death, that is. [I always laugh at Martin's reply.]

JC: Did you get my letter with the DeLillo and Saul Bellow clippings? I know you like them. DeLillo says if you are complaining, by gum, you better be entertaining about it. If you are neurotic, you have to make it interesting. Of course, my own neuroses are always interesting to me.

MA: That's the trouble.

JC: Oscar Wilde said women go on and on complaining about something they have no control over, and I get caught up in that myself, especially in PMS—premenstrual syndrome. It's perfectly odious, and I should lock myself up.

MA: We call it PMT ... for tension.

JC: In America, we say PMS stands for "Permissible Man Slaughter." (Martin is aghast for a second, like most men when they hear the acronym's ulterior definition.) Why do you know so much about it? My boyfriend thinks I'm just giving him an excuse to be reprehensible. How do you understand it?

MA: I regard it as riding the hormone. The other part is that you don't know you're being odious at the time. It all seems suddenly justified. And a couple of days later, you think, — Christ!

JC: (laughing) May I quote you?

MA: Sure. You ride that hormone. Anyone knows who's busted steers that if you let the horse have the strength, it tires itself out because if you come up against it, you've had it. Let it beat itself out.

JC: Do you consider yourself androgynous?

MA: Yeah. If you have any power of imagination, then you've got to see it's a different deal, being a woman. Now that's going to get me into a lot of trouble, saying that.

JC: Not with me, because it's true. Vive la difference.

MA: I know in my heart that it's the case. I know that anyone who says opposite is talking bullshit. I've had plenty of experiences of PMS from the other end.

JC: You mean from women?

MA: Yeah.

JC: But don't you hate them when they're like that?

MA: Not really. I just think, Jesus, how long is this going to last?

Martin in his writing flat

• • •

Lost in London: How Did I Get Here?

Our first meeting and interview ended around 5:00 pm when London was getting dark and Martin had to go home to have dinner with his family. I thanked him for inviting me to his flat and for the interview.

Visiting Martin Amis

He invited me to come back in a week to continue the interview. Of course, I was delighted we would meet again the following Monday. In the meantime, I could see more of London, take in more stage plays in the theater district, and book a tour bus to Stonehenge.

Martin walked me down the narrow, winding staircase to the door and told me I could get a taxi at the corner. Well, that wasn't the case. Granted, I was exhilarated from meeting Martin Amis and being in London, and was mildly exhilarated as I walked outside. Unknowingly, I turned the opposite way on Leamington Road Villas from where I had arrived. After walking a few blocks in drizzling rain, I didn't see any available taxis in the by-now-dark night. I walked farther to a busy street crowded with people getting off work and waiting for buses to catch. This area of West London was flooded with sketchy-looking pedestrians, and roaming, young men. I realized finally that I didn't know where I was. The London December drizzle turned to rain. I was cold, drenched, and alone.

Crossing back and forth over streets, I certainly looked lost. Still, there were no taxis, only buses splashing water as they buzzed by. Now the rain was coming down hard, and I didn't have an umbrella. I was a sorry soul in the downpour. Wet and cold, I began to be apprehensive because I knew I looked out of place and vulnerable in my mink jacket, skirt, and high heels. My Louis bag hung from my shoulder over my wet hair.

Young men of various complexion shades, looking like they had nothing to lose, stared at me, sensing I didn't belong; what was *she* doing here? Later I read a review of *London Fields* by John Lahr in *Vogue* (April 1990) who wrote:

"The name Amis, barely legible has been scratched under the bell of a ramshackle Victorian house in Notting Hill, few blocks from the notorious All Saints Road, with its drug-dealing villains, and a little farther from the louche mix that is Portobello Road, where the wealthy and the wretched bump up against each other as they scavenge for pleasure."

From what I distinctly remember, I had to be in what Lahr had described as the "the notorious All Saints Road, with its drug-dealing villains, …"

After walking another three or four blocks in the pouring rain with no luck finding a taxi, I stood on a corner and waited for the next bus to stop. When one did, I got in, showed the driver my transit pass, and sat down in the first available seat. Riding the bus up and down unknown streets, not knowing where it was going, I asked a nearby passenger where Lansdowne Road was. Once on it, I knew my cousin's address and could walk to his house.

Hearing my American accent, two ladies on the bus came to my rescue and showed me where to get off on Lansdowne Road. When I saw the address numbers were a long way from my cousin's, I had to walk a dozen more, rain-soaked blocks to his house. Finally, I saw Owen's street number, opened the iron-wrought gate and rang the doorbell.

Karen opened the door to find me shivering, wet, cold, and exhausted, but relieved to be home.

• • •

Four

Killing a Week in London

If you have a week to kill in any city in the world, London is the place to do it. At least it was in the 1980's. I decided to see as much of the world's spectacular town as I could squeeze into seven days. When my week at the Bloomsbury hotel was over, my cousin Owen graciously invited me to stay with his wife and two boys in their three-story townhouse in the high-end, West London neighborhood of Notting Hill. When I had gotten lost after the first interview with Martin, I didn't know my cousin's house on Lansdowne Road was within walking distance to Martin's studio on Leamington Road Villas, or I could have saved myself a lot of stress.

After thanking Owen and Karen for inviting me to stay in their lovely home, I moved in to explore London from there. I started out walking in the early morning to the Notting Hill Gate Underground station and boarded the Tube to Piccadilly Circus. Karen told me a ticket booth in Piccadilly Square sold tickets at half-price for available seats on the day's theater performances.

During that week I bought several tickets for both matinee and evening shows. My favorite play was *A Man for All Seasons*, starring Charlton Heston as Sir Thomas More, Chancellor to King Henry VIII. For the matinee performance, I sat in the middle of the second row in an almost empty theatre, pretending the film star of *Ben Hur, The*

Ten Commandments, and *Planet of the Apes* was performing Sir Thomas for my singular enjoyment. (In a way, in the absent theater, he was.) I thought Heston's performance of Sir Thomas More was better than Paul Scofield's, who had won the Oscar for Best Actor in the film.

Like the British writers James Boswell, Oscar Wilde, and Charles Dickens, London, England—with all its fabulous sights and forgivable misdeeds—became my favorite city in the world. It had everything Los Angeles did not—a prolonged, millennia history, classical architecture from past eras, and Shakespeare's resurrected Globe Theater, which performed his plays nightly. Sophisticated culture filled the eye and ear everywhere—whereas L.A. had the nouveau riche, extravagance, materialism, superhero action films, and our pervasive American pop culture.

London's roots went back two thousand years to the Roman conquest of Britannia in 43 AD, when Caesar's centurions founded the city on the Thames River as a Roman fortress on the large island. Roman soldiers constructed a city of brick and mortar, the dilapidated walls of which can be seen partly standing today. I walked over London's cobblestone streets hand-laid centuries ago; and looked up to see byzantine carvings and gargoyles looming out from medieval buildings to frighten off demons.

London has been rebuilt several times over the millennia. The Black Death arrived in Britain from diseased fleas carried by rats on cargo ships from Asia in the autumn of 1348, and by late spring the following year, the bubonic plague had killed six out of every ten people in London. Continuous, bloody wars raged between the Norman and Saxon nobles; Celtic tribes fought to keep their lands as they ravaged the countryside against invaders; and centuries of religious wars between British royalists. The Great London Fire of 1666 consumed the entire city. In mid–twentieth century World War II, the Nazis blitzkrieg raids bombed London into piles of mortar, bricks, and cinderblock on the streets.

Now London was bustling with commerce and merchants as it did during the renaissance of Elizabeth I and in HRH Victoria's empiric reign. Its thriving business, companies, and international banking have made London one of the most prosperous cities in the world. London is a shoppers' paradise with elegant department stores and antique shops, markets and wares on Portobello Road and collectable merchandise in Covent Gardens; multiple flea markets are found throughout the city to rummage and bargain on a treasure. If ever I fell in love with a city, it was London.

I spent an entire day at the National Gallery museum where I saw the masterpieces by great Renaissance artists, Leonardo da Vinci, Michelangelo, Titian, Rafael, Botticelli, and Caravaggio; the Flemish masters, Rembrandt, Rubens, Holbein, van Dyck, and Vermeer; and famous paintings by French Impressionists, Renoir, Vincent van Gogh, Claude Monet, Pizarro, and Manet among hundreds.

Walking along the aisles of paintings by English artists, Gainsborough and Turner into the other galleries, which featured the modern artists of the early 20th century, Picasso, Matisse, and Duchamp. It was thrilling to see portraits of the royal Spanish families by court painters, Goya, El Greco, and Velasquez that I had only seen in art classes at UCLA. The day at the National Gallery was well spent among its invaluable, genius art.

The next day I visited Queen Victoria and Prince Albert Museum (seven-pound donation). A sign read: "*The world's largest museum of decorative arts and design, housing a permanent collection of over 4.5 million objects.*" Ceiling-tall rooms were filled with foreign treasures that British ships had confiscated and brought back from Asian lands referred to as 'the Orient'— Egypt, Jordan, Iraq, Iran, and Syria, to the Far East Orient: India, China, Japan, the Spice Islands–wherever the English captains docked their ships in faraway East. An entire floor is dedicated to a millennium of English kings and queens from King Ethelred the Unready and William the Conqueror in 1066, to the eponymous age of Queen Elizabeth 1, to HRH Queen Victoria and Prince Albert until HRM's long reign ended in 1901 when she died.

Miles of aisles of medieval weapons and treasure despoiled from wars by many English kings' armies and conquests in their internecine, religious wars were displayed in continuous, giant halls and chambers. Scores of medieval knights shining armor and lances shone from protruding rafters. The Golden Age of Couture exhibited historical fashion representing three hundred years of costume and sartorial dress in the V and A. It would take days to see it all.

When I didn't go to the theater in the evening, I went on London walking tours—the Tower of London, the haunts of the Shakespeare's Old Globe Theatre and Charles Dickens novels; Conan Doyle's *Sherlock Holmes* address on Baker Street, and miles of black, cobblestone alleyways that transported time back to merry, but dirty, old London. I went twice on the Jack the Ripper tour; this time with a different guide who didn't spare one lurid, bloody detail. (For those who have the stomach, unedited photos of the mutilated corpses of female victims that Jack sliced apart in his wake can be seen online.) The crusty, old guide walked our small group of five Americans, including a couple with their teenage son, around the maroon brick streets to the exact alleys and boardinghouse room where Jack viciously stabbed and methodically dissected the body of his last lady.

When we walked across moss-covered graves on a dilapidated church ground, our guide told us the Black Plague in the fourteenth century had taken more than half the lives of London's medieval population. He explained that the afflicted died slowly—starting with a fever, chills, pains in the groin and swollen lymph nodes, nonstop vomiting of green bile, followed by purulent black boils that oozed pus over their rag-soaked bodies.

I chimed in, "It sounds kind of like menopause." Everyone including the teenager laughed.

The City of London Museum showcased the history of prehistoric man in Great Britain. Near the museum entrance, I saw a sign pointing to a Roman City wall that Caesar's soldiers had constructed with bricks and mortar; it was still partially standing. Ordered by Roman Emperor Claudius, a Roman army invaded the British Isles in 43 AD when only disparate, indigenous Celts lived within small tribes disconnected from one another. Glass-encased exhibits showed models of Celtic tribes in the Stone Age with roughly hewed flint spears, knives, and artifacts. These Neolithic ancestors of today's Brits and Anglo-Saxons survived in makeshift, animal hide tents, using primitive tools and weapons for hunting and cooking. Exhibits also displayed models of earlier, prehistoric hominoids—the Neanderthals—dwelling in caves and hunting with crude spears and wood cudgels. The physiognomy of the simian-like Neanderthals was distinguishingly different from larger-brained Homo sapiens who arrived later—roughly forty thousand years ago. Neanderthals eventually died out, but not before Homo sapiens reached Europe and the British Isles.

Research reveals that Neanderthals became extinct thousands of years after Homo sapiens arrived. The recent migrants survived due to superior brains and hunting skills. Anthropologists now report that Neanderthals were still extant—if not thriving in Europe—when Homo sapiens appeared, and coexisted with them for millennia. I wondered if the two species procreated.

I asked a museum security guard standing at a wall, "Did Homo sapiens interbreed with Neanderthals?"

He said he would ask his supervisor and disappeared behind a free-standing wall. A few moments later, he reappeared and answered a decisive "No."

However, according to current anthropological evidence, this is not true. Through rigorous genetic testing, anthropologists today maintain that all people of European descent have between 1 and 3 percent Neanderthal DNA in their cellular genome. This physical evidence proves that sexual contact between the prehistoric Neanderthal and Homo sapiens man resulted in a hybrid human offspring that shows up in modern DNA testing. Ψ Eventually, the Neanderthals, Homo erectus, and other prehistoric hominoids eventually died out, outlived by mentally and physically superior Homo sapiens. Darwin's theory—Survival of the fittest— supports the hearty emergence of prehistoric Europeans. Ever since Homo sapiens have reigned over the natural world.

I felt a *joie vivre* the entire time in London experiencing its long history, rich culture, outstanding theater and art. I was alive in the German philosopher, Heidegger's *Dasein*—the existential, human experience of being present in the world.

Ψ "It is not known when they first met Neanderthals, but at least once, in one location, there was a positive outcome—for genetic evidence suggests some interbreeding took place between the species. As a result, tiny fragments of Neanderthal DNA live on in our genes." www.guardian.co.uk/science/2013/jun/two/

London Trafalgar Square

• • •

My cousins knew about my interview with Martin Amis and that he had invited me to come back next Monday to continue. Karen said she had bought Martin's novel, *Success* (1984), for Owen. Their youngest son, Jaime, age ten, was in Martin's son's class at public school. My cousins had enrolled their sons in the same public school as Amis's sons, since both families lived in the same Notting Hill neighborhood. (In England, public school is the same as our private school.)

"Martin's wife stopped by one day to pick up Jaime to go to a school program with her son, and I met her."

"What did she look like?" I asked.

"She's an attractive." Karen said, adding, "She seemed to be a good mother to her boys."

Karen could relate to Martin's wife who had two young boys at the same school and lived in the area. (I didn't know at the time they would eventually share more in common.) I stayed the week with my cousin on Lansdowne Road until my next meeting with Martin. The fact that their house was a convenient walk to his writing flat was among several coincidences I was to encounter in London.

During the week I took the Tube at Notting Hill Gate to whatever tourist attraction I decided on. One day, I spent three hours in Harrods department store and then boarded the Underground to the Riverside Station to purchase a ride on the Thames River cruise to Greenwich Maritime Museum. I remember the biting, wet cold stinging my face on the deck of the boat where I chose to sit instead of inside the warmer cabin. As usual, the drizzly London winter rain came and went continuously in brief, ten minute showers. I've always found rain refreshing (except when I can't escape it, like the night I got lost after leaving Martin's flat). The temperature didn't drop below forty degrees Fahrenheit, so I was warm inside my wool coat, shawl, and leather boots as I walked miles and miles from morning until night all over London. The walking tours were especially memorable because the genial guides told colorful stories about merry, old London. Many out-of-work actors made the guided walks entertaining and educational as well as earning money between acting jobs.

Running around London and its endless attractions sometimes overshadowed the thought of my next interview with Martin. The city's magnificent sights and historical buildings were spectacular, but in the back of my mind, I knew I'd soon be with him again. I didn't have any particular agenda or intention brewing in my empty head regarding the fascinating writer I would be alone with. All I knew was Monday would come, and Martin would captivate my entire attention. I didn't give Greg, my boyfriend in L.A., a second thought, except once when I was visiting Stonehenge, an hour's bus ride out of London.

Standing before the circular 3000 BC Stonehenge monuments on the Salisbury Plain was surreal to me. Awestruck, I stared at the prehistoric, twenty-five-ton stone pillars for an unforgettable five minutes; many of the five thousand year old pillars were still standing—some topped by eroded, original lintels. In the Stonehenge gift shop, I bought Greg a book on Celtic symbols and artifacts. He often incorporated cultural symbols in his art and might copy the hand-carved hilt of a Celtic sword in a work. Putting the art book in the museum gift bag, my body returned to London and my mind to Martin Amis.

Five

The Information Is Delivered: The Interview Part 2

*"The end of the world is saying, 'It's possible.
Take your pick, bang or whimper.'"*

— Martin Amis

Monday finally came, and I was again sitting on a sofa across from Martin Amis in his writing flat. I felt fortunate to be with this unique author who had the potential to be a hallmark of modern literature. Martin always maintained that it's posterity that will decide whether or not his writing stands up to the distinction. Will his novels be read in the last half of the twenty-first century, or will they be confined to an obscure shelf of literary history?

I noticed the clothes Martin wore this time in comparison to what he had been wearing the week before. At our first meeting, Martin had had on a black T-shirt and blue jeans; whereas I had come more dressed up in a designer wool skirt and sweater, black hose, suede pumps, and mink jacket. In contrast this time I had dressed down to match his casual style in fitted jeans and a cashmere sweater, while Martin was dressed in trousers, a white, dress shirt, and black vest. Apparently, we had both noticed our obverse sartorial styles from the week before. I asked if I could take photos with my disposable camera and he agreed.

Martin in his studio

Martin sensed that I had warmed up to him and had adjusted to his appearance in person. The impact of his story, "Insight at Flame Lake," that I had read in *Vanity Fair* that spring had compelled me to fly across America and the Atlantic Ocean to meet the author. Fate had given me the opportunity to interview him; so now, face-to-face, I wanted to explore the uniqueness of Martin Amis and his unorthodox mind. I needed to understand what the short story meant that had pierced the heart of my heart last summer. So I began the second interview with it.

Visiting Martin Amis

J. Clinch: I know you had a fascination with science fiction as a young man, and you incorporated it in the story, "Insight at Flame Lake," which is about a schizophrenic boy whose brilliant father committed suicide. Is this anyone you know?

Martin Amis: No, his name is Dan. He wasn't based on anyone. A story emerged, which, as often happens, when three threads come together and you realize you have a story you can write. But, in fact, it's difficult to base characters on real people, even if desirable, because they don't fit into the novel.

JC: Okay, and three things come together in your life?

MA: I was just on holiday in Cape Cod near a big lake, as they call them there, a pond. We would call it a lake here in England because of the scale of things there in America. A pond is just a bit bigger than a puddle and a lake is anything bigger than two feet across. It was very hot, and I was reading a book about schizophrenia, and there was a baby present—mine—the older boy, and there was this nuclear matter in the back of my mind, and that's the heart of the story. Also...who wrote *Psycho*? I think it's Don Block. There is a horror story he wrote after *Psycho* about a wretched baby in an anthology collection edited by him. I just thought if things come together and then the boy would see evil in a baby, although no evil was there. As a result, the huge distortion foisted on us by the nuclear reality; I mean, that's making it sound more exact than when I was writing it, but it was along those lines.

JC: What experience have you had with schizophrenia?

MA: I've known, I guess everyone's known two or three people who've suffered from it from one extent to another.

JC: How do you know? Were they diagnosed?

MA: Yeah, and you hear that they are.

JC: Your grasp of the disease blew me across the room as I read 'Flame Lake.' Do you know R. D. Laing and his books about schizophrenia?

MA: Yeah. But I don't agree with his theory. Laing said it is an enlightening experience. I don't think he treats it as the dismal experience it really is.

JC: I love when Dan says, "Reality is out of control," and "The reality problem is always ready to explode." Where did you come up with that? It's so true.

MA: It's the literal truth of the nuclear age. It's actually the case. Dan is quite right there. I'm not a Laingian, but Dan is seeing the truth when he says that.

JC: Why do you say you're not a Laingian?

MA: Because I believe that to call the insane, "sane", insults the insane because they're having too bad a time.

JC: The first time I came to London, I was looking for R. D. Laing. I was twenty-two and had just graduated from UCLA and immediately had a culture shock. It stemmed from several philosophy courses I had taken in my senior year in existentialism and phenomenology. John Stuart Mill had the same experience when he graduated from an English college, but they called his condition "a severe emotional crisis." But then, he's a bit different from me. I admit, smiling.

MA: Alienation can happen to people in a life crisis when all that global rationality you've been getting along with isn't enough anymore. Maybe the idea that you're going to die is really sinking in. We fended off for so long.

JC: I remember distinctly during my breakdown when I realized I was mortal, and it shocked me explosively at the age of twenty-two. How old were you when you realized you were mortal?

MA: Not until the other day—if indeed, then, last week sometime.

JC: (laughing) Come on now…seriously.

MA: I think the first time when I saw some Davy Crockett-type film, and a guy got it in the back with the bayonet. I thought, Christ, he's really dead! I was about eight when I realized there were endings. There's a nice little cameo in Saul Bellow's book about Israel where he's going up stairs with an eighty-one-year-old guy, and he's helping him upstairs, and the old man is a very energetic, old philanthropist who says, "Well, you know, eighty-one is not eighteen, but all this is getting old, as far as I'm concerned, it's just a rumor."

JC: (laughs) You mean he's never accepted it?

MA: I don't think people really take it on board. That must be something profoundly human. What separates us from animals is knowing we're going to die. It seems it would be intolerable if we took it on board—that were going to die.

JC: That was my big concern at twenty-two. And I wanted to know why was I on the third planet from the sun?

MA: That's really a very good question.

JC: I read Albert Camus, who said that the whole life experience was absurd because it's temporal. That didn't help any.

MA: I think middle age is a little rehearsal for death.

JC: Really? What makes you say that?

MA: There's little reminders every day. Every time you bend down to pick something up, you find yourself groaning and you think, who said that? And then you realize it's you. I play tennis a lot, and every so often, I jump up for an overhead and I land awkwardly, then I go on playing. But then, the next day I can't walk. Or I play squash, and the next day I can't move my neck.

JC: Isn't it funny that a man would experience middle age as a physical thing? With a woman, it's more something you feel inside.

MA: It's an emotional discovery for you.

JC: Like that Saul Bellow fellow, I saw death as something that happened to other people…like grandfathers. I was so alive. I couldn't conceive of it happening to me!

MA: All the evidence suggests it will happen to everyone, but not to us. (We both laugh.)

JC: The worst part is these damn French existentialists saying, "Why bother? Life is absurd." Then Camus advised, if you must live, *s'engager*—that is, engage yourself in some kind of work or passion. I still don't know what I'm going to do when I grow up.

MA: Even if you do grow up and you do what grown-ups do, I don't think you ever feel that different in your soul.

JC: Really?

MA: Tolstoy said something like we don't grow in time, that time just moves us while inside we remain the same, which is a deeply somber view.

JC: You mean we really don't change?

MA: Not in the soul or in the heart. Only time passing has any effect on us and makes us look and feel older. Ψ

JC: Don't you think we mature and learn lessons in life?

MA: Oh, sure we do. I blushed for my younger self.

JC: Don't we all?

MA: Yeah. Sometimes we have to fight off the memory—even make a noise, so it will go away.

JC: I envy those people who had blackouts and couldn't remember anything they've done—like when they were drunk.

MA: I think a lot of that blackout stuff is faked.

JC: Really? They say it's possible to have brain synapses break down.

MA: I'm sure there are degrees, but I'm also sure they say they can't remember and then as long as you think they can't remember…

JC: How can they do that? Am I just neurotically honest?

MA: Something like that.

• • •

I Lost It at the Movies

— PAULINE KAEL, FILM CRITIC, *THE NEW YORKER*

Ψ In twenty-five years, Martin Amis contradicted this: "Every ten years you're a different person, and the really great books evolve with you as you get older. They're full of new rewards." Our Man in Brooklyn" by John Heilpern. *Vanity Fair* Sept. 2012.

Visiting Martin Amis

Because we both were film buffs, I wanted to talk to Martin about movies and actors. Gossiping about films and celebrities is fun between like-minded people. If one of us liked an actor the other did not, one usually had the courtesy not to point out the actor was over-rated, if not a complete *artiste manqué.*

"I know you like De Niro and Martin Scorsese, especially *Raging Bull.* I heard Scorsese say the film was more about redemption. I'm not Catholic, but I have a certain attraction that draws me to redemption. I was raised in the Puget Sound with lots of working-class stock—except they don't really have classes there, per se." [5]

Martin replied, "Lucky you."

"Your class lines are much more defined here. I read you asked your dad when you were young if you were nouveau riche, and he said, 'We are very *nouveau,* but not very *riche.*' "

"Yeah," Martin said. "It shattered me."

I laughed, and then continued about Scorsese. "Why do you like *Raging Bull?*"

"I'm surprised Scorsese said it was a film about redemption, because that's exactly what it isn't," Martin stated. "Jake LaMotta is completely unredeemable."

"I heard Scorsese say that during an interview."

"Well, then, it's about missed redemption in that case."

I ventured, "Maybe it's about a man who's trying to redeem himself."

Martin quickly replies, "Well, he's not trying very hard."

"Really? But he pays for it. Remember when he hits himself against his prison cell wall?"

"Yeah, that was a great scene, a startling, extraordinary scene. But LaMotta ends up reciting those lines from *On the Waterfront.*"

---

5 This is not true. Of course, we have social classes in America. I was comparing the class distinctions in British society vs. those in America, which are based on wealth: Old Money vs. New Money; work, etc.: Reference: Paul Fussell, *Class, A Guide Through the American Status System.* New York: Simon & Schuster. Note: Paul Fussell was a close army friend of Martin's father; he wrote *The Anti-Egoist: Kingsley Amis, Man of Letters.* Oxford University Press 1994

"'I could'a been a contender, I could'a had class.'" I recited.

Martin continued, "Yeah, that's right because he's still blaming his brother, 'You were my brother. You should'a looked after me.' And the film ends with a dedication to his teacher, saying he had redeemed himself—Scorsese did. But Jake LaMotta is left shadow-dancing and degrading himself."

"Maybe that's the redemption." I pondered. "Or it's just irony. He was old and wasted. The self-flagellation for having been a wretched drunk, whatever it is that makes us despair and hate ourselves...like when Jake hits his head on the cement wall."

Martin repeated Jake's cries, "I'm not an animal! I'm not an animal!"...

"Remember at that nightclub—which is brilliantly written—when all the jokes are on himself? Like when Jake says, 'When I came here tonight, they showed me to my dressing room,' and I asked, 'Where's the toilet?' And they said, 'You're in it.' Very self-degrading jokes in his act."

"That's decisively why I think he knows it was himself to blame—not his brother—for his failure as a human being," I argued, "And that's why he hits his head against the wall."

"Sure, but that's just an illusion of foolish rage," Martin said.

"Rage? I saw it as self-hatred."

Martin claimed, "It's self-disgust. But he doesn't come out of it. It's hard to imagine a redemption ending to the film. Jake's not going to work with any children or anything."

"I don't know what he's doing now in real life."

"Me, neither, and I read the book, too." Martin added.

"When Scorsese admitted it was about redemption, he meant his own redemption. Do we ever redeem ourselves from our sins?" I asked.

"Scorsese makes some funny implications about himself in the film." Martin said. "He's certainly a scurrilous, scruffy-looking guy. Remember in *Taxi Driver* when he played the husband spying on his ex-wife's apartment in the back of De Niro's cab?" Martin repeats Scorsese's line: "Do you know what a forty-five magnum can do to a woman's pussy?"

"How could you forget that?" I abashedly blurted.

"Well, he's a genius." Martin reminded me.

"You said it."

"I don't know how articulate he is, but he sounds like a giggly mute. He's incredibly oppressive about modern times. I think he's on to great themes."

Then Martin asked, "Uh, for instance, how do you interpret the end of *Taxi Driver*?"

"It's about a man who wants to assassinate the president, like John Hinckley or Oswald, but he turns out to be a hero. It's a reversal in life—like *peripeteia*, a reversal that occurs toward the end in a Greek play. It's what you said about reality being out of control."

Martin explained, "According to Scorsese, all that blasting after he's shot is sort of a dead fantasy, a dream. It's what's going through his head when he's dying that he's been redeemed. There is the letter from Jodie Foster's parents."

"Isn't that the redemption?"

"But it's false," Martin said, "because it's just a dream in a squalid death in a brothel. In fact, he's dying, and it's a last-wish fulfillment that he's redeemed. He gives a lift to Cybil Shepherd, and everything's OK."

"That's an illusion?" I am surprised. "You mean, in reality he's been killed in the shoot out?"

"He's dead. They kill him. That's what Scorsese said."

I recounted what I'd read in *The New Yorker*. "Film critic, Pauline Kael, said Catholic directors like Scorsese, Fellini, and Brian De Palma express their dramatic themes in vibrant colors, blood-red, passionate sex; redemption, heaven and hell. Whereas Protestant and Jewish directors are methodical; they make black-and-white films, or even dark and turgid ones like the Swedish director, Ingmar Bergman and Stanley Kubrick."

Martin agreed. "Yeah, it's all very bold and operatic…particularly De Palma."

"Talk about a misogynist." I chimed in.

"He loves to hack women up."

"I never forgave him for putting Michael Caine in drag in *Dressed to Kill.* You can't compare him to Scorsese."

"Oh no." Martin quickly added. "He's not in the same class. Have you seen my book of journalism, *The Moronic Inferno*?"

"I read it."

"Di Palma is a likable megalomaniac."

I ask, "He put you off a bit, did he?"

"He screwed me around. I have to admit I sort of liked him in the end."

(I interrupted Martin because at this point, I was shivering from a draft coming from an open window. I turned around, saw the cold creeping in, and asked Martin to please close the nearby window. Martin chuckled as he got up and closed it. I told him I wasn't used to London's chilly, damp weather, since I had just arrived from sunny Southern California.)

JC: Did De Palma grow on you?

MA: He did eventually.

JC: I don't see De Palma as charming.

MA: No, he wasn't, definitely not. But he exuded a sort of charm, the non-discreet charm. He's char-ish and loud and forthright, sort of in an enjoyable way.

JC: Sigmund Freud said, "Money and beauty are the only two values left this world." Do you agree?

MA: (repeating the words) ... Money and beauty. Well, it's hard to give a yes or no to that. I'd say money is certainly riding high at the moment of value.

JC: At the moment? I saw some gold coins at the British Museum today, and they were in circulation thousands of years BC.

MA: It's always been up there. There is more candor about money now. Reagan called it "the new opulence." I think "shamelessness" is more like it.

JC: Well, you see it a lot of it in my town (Beverly Hills, California).

Your story in *Einstein's Monsters* talks about beauty, "The Little Puppy That Could." And everyone has time for beauty, for art. We all come around to beauty in the end. Wasn't beauty what ingratiated the little puppy when it was actually the antichrist?

MA: Sure, but what interests me is how do we get our agreement about what is beautiful? Where does it come from? Why people agree it's nicer to look at Sophia Loren than Margaret Thatcher? What are our guidelines for this?

JC: It's changed throughout the centuries—basically, it's about proportion. At least that's what Aristotle said.

MA: Some people say what makes a woman appealing is resemblance to a baby…largeness of eyes.

JC: A wide face, roundness. Which brings me to inquire about your obsession with babies—you have one, you know—with them.

MA: Only recently.

JC: Well, I'm going to cite examples of why I said that: Rosa is a baby, for one, in a short story, and it's the title of your second novel, *Dead Babies*, and the baby, Harriet, who's a central character in "Flame Lake." Also, you said there are two babies in your next novel who are polar opposites of each other.   (Like your little boys? I wondered.)

MA: It's only after having a couple [of babies]. It opens up the cast of characters.

JC: Rachel said, "Women can have babies, men can't," in *The Rachel Papers*. That's a truism, but you seem to dwell on it. Anyway, my guess it's a bias you have with procreation, an envy that women can reproduce—a superiority.

MA: I always write about extremes; the two babies in my book that's on the typewriter now—one is a little bundle of heaven—the other's a little bundle of hell.

JC: Devil and angel.

MA: And they're both…in each. *London Fields* has two babies in it who are both heaven and hell. They're a nightmare, but they're also a gorgeous dream at the same time. I separate them out because that's what I usually do in my fiction; pile all the noxious characteristics on the one.

JC: Like little Keith Whitehead, yuck!

MA: Exactly. Quite yuck. I wanted people to hate him, but many had a soft spot for him.

JC: Because he's so pathetic. People love the underdog.

MA: That's right. I thought I'd made the character as physically reprehensible as possible, also nasty.

JC: No redeeming qualities.

MA: But a lot of people, especially women, felt protective of him.

JC: Well, I didn't, because I've known creeps like that who are repulsive. Some become very rich and surround themselves with young girls… teenagers. (I cited an example of a famous dirty old man in Hollywood.)

MA: He is a little Keith, isn't he?

JC: Oh, you heard of him? (I was surprised Martin knew of this L.A. character's infamy.) There are a lot of little Keith's in real life. It must be terrible to be that repulsive-looking and entice girls to sleep with you, knowing they are doing it for some ulterior reward or money. Some women feel sorry for this type. Or they have a feeling of superiority over him, but he's just exploiting them.

MA: There is the mother instinct, too.

JC: They think somebody has to love them.

MA: Yeah. As for the babies, I divide up good and bad. I give all the good to one and the bad to the other.

JC: The black-and-white extreme?

MA: Yes, the nice baby sleeps and is good—never sick, and the other…

JC: The other is Damien, with three sixes on his head.

MA: Exactly. Six–six–six. The older boy is the wicked one. In "The Puppy That Could," it's the same thing. You make the puppy so cute, you want to hug him forever, and you make the dog explosively repulsive.

JC: Yeah, she ate people just for fun and then at the end, the little puppy became her son?

MA: Her lover. He's given a sort of magical nature setting—he has gone crazy on a wave of evolution—is risen from the ashes, Phoenix-like.

JC: That's an interesting concept, "The Little Puppy That Could." Could what?

MA: Could do it! "The Little Engine That Could!" All the trains said he couldn't, and he did!

JC: You like these decisive characters.

MA: They're more grotesque.

JC: Do you have a fascination with the macabre?

MA: Not really.

JC: Because Emma Sands called you a little Keith in her article on you.

MA: I know, but that was a joke started by me. She still does when she rings up and says, "Little Keith?"

JC: It's a joke on yourself?

MA: Yeah, it's one of my pseudonyms.

JC: Why is Keith Whitehead such a terrible name?

MA: Because it's a kind of pimple.

JC: (I laugh at this.) It's a common English name. Wasn't there a British philosopher named Whitehead, too?

MA: There is a Member of Parliament, Whitehead.

JC: I still can't get over the coincidence that my name—Clinch—is a character in your current novel.

MA: Freaks you, does it?

JC: Yes, it's staggering. Who is Guy Clinch in your novel?

MA: The protagonist—a genuine sweetie.

JC: Then I don't like him already. (I kidded.)

MA: It's hard to make a character interesting if they are too nice. He's slightly weak.

JC: That makes him all the more repugnant. Who likes weak men?

MA: He's not meant to be a big heartthrob, although he's sort of beautiful to look at. He's upper class—he has a sort of weakness with that.

JC: Because of his blue blood?

MA: And plus his niceness, and that screws him up. He's rich and he can't cope with that.

JC: I had a boyfriend once who was that way. I used to say, "He was very well bred; he had too much blue blood, not enough red." He was too weak from my feisty temperament.

MA: What did he do?

JC: He came from a wealthy family who lived in Laguna Beach—a high end, beachfront area in Southern California. He did what he wanted—to his father's disappointment—which was to play bass guitar. He traveled on tour with Ray Charles. Eventually I got him work at Universal Studios. Last I heard he was working full time for Universal's music department. How far along are you into your novel?

MA: I shall have to start typing the final draft. I've finished it, and there are huge holes in it. I'll do it on the typewriter. I've got to get it finished by next year because I want it to come out in 1989. If it gets into 1990, it'll be too close to the time it's centered, the millennium. It'll be out in September 1989. It's roughly on schedule. (Martin pronounced the word shed-ual. We Yanks pronounce the hard c—like sked'yule.)

JC: For a good film, Martin, you have to see *Barfly*. It's about the renegade, L.A. poet-author, Charles Bukowski.

MA: I love Mickey Rourke. He's a bit hit and miss, but when he's good, he's really delicious. I loved the film, *The Pope of Greenwich Village*.

JC: Why that one?

MA: I think it's a great film. I loved the book. I think he and Eric Roberts had a great thing going. Eric said, "He took my thumb. The big thug took my thumb." Remember that?

JC: Yeah. Anyway, Rourke drinks beer in this outside café in Beverly Hills in the afternoon.

MA: He's a barfly. (An astute observation, but I am talking with a brainiac.)

JC: He really is! When I last saw him in the bar, I asked him what he thought of Bukowski, and he said he didn't care for him too much because when he was growing up, his uncles were always drunk, and Bukowski reminded him of his drunken uncles who trashed the house and abused his mother, so he didn't like him.

MA: Did he make him sympathetic in the film?

JC: Yes, he makes him likable. Do you like him? Bukowski—played by Rourke—is always in a bar fight in the movie. I like what he says in the film. I identified with some of Bukowski's ideas, like when he says: "There's so many places in the world you're supposed to want to go to. Everybody's telling you, you have to be somebody, you have to do something!" Bukowski complains, "There are so many places I *don't* want to go to. There's so many things I *don't* want to do." That struck a chord with me because I don't want to either.

You said you were going to see Adam Brooks next week who's directing *Money*. I'm an actress—do you think there's anything in the script I could be right for?

MA: Leave a photo, and I'll be happy to give it to him with a good recommendation.

JC: Thanks, Martin. I appreciate it.

It was around five o'clock when Martin said he had to pick up his boys from school and go home, so we ended the interview. As we were leaving, I told him I'd gotten lost after our last interview and that it had taken me hours to get to my cousin's home on Lansdowne Road about a mile away. When he heard how close it was, Martin offered to drive me back to their house.

Arriving at my cousin's gate, Martin expressed what a lovely house it was, nestled between rose bushes and other three storied, ironed-gated townhouses on the charming, West London street. [6] We said goodbye and Martin added, "Let's stay in touch," and promised to write.

When Karen opened the door, I told her Martin Amis had just dropped me off. I felt a kind of euphoria—*Dasein* again—vibrantly alive in the world

---

6 The scene in the film *Notting Hill* where Julia Roberts and Hugh Grant stroll around a garden was shot in the communal garden behind my cousin's West London house on Lansdowne Road. Note: The Lansdowne area is where Guy Clinch lives in the novel, *London Fields*.

Six

BACK TO BEVERLY HILLS

I flew back home to LAX from London pleased I'd accomplished my goal of meeting and interviewing Martin Amis. I had more than two hours of taped interviews on cassettes I would transcribe to text on my IBM Selectric 2 typewriter. I didn't discuss my experience in London with my boyfriend, Greg, but I did tell him I had gotten the interview and planned to send it to a literary magazine. Greg said that Ed Ruscha's one-man show at the Leo Castelli Gallery in New York City had sold out. Art collectors and museums bought all of Ruscha's exhibited paintings.

I called Martin in London to tell him it was delightful meeting him and to thank him again for the interview. He reciprocated in kind. During the month since my return, we talked a few times on the phone; then I received a letter from London the week before Christmas.

The envelope and letter were written by hand in Martin's fountain pen. *The Observer* stationery headline showed an escutcheon flanked by a lion with a man's head and a unicorn, topped by the royal crown, underscored "Established 1791." The medallion read: *Honi Soit Qui Mal y Pense.* Written beneath the lion and unicorn were the French words, *Dieu et Mon Droit. The Observer*'s address, phone number, and Registration were printed below the medallion, and the company directors were listed on the bottom.

The envelope was postmarked 18 December 1987 in London addressed to my apartment in Beverly Hills, California. Martin wrote that he was seeing Adam Brooks, the director of the film, *Money,* but didn't think I was suitable for either role of the two female leads. I was too young for Butch, and Selena was English; plus her role would demand a lot of nudity—"exhausting nudity," in fact. (*Pas moi.*)

Martin was happy to hear that I had a good time in London. He added he loved 'this Clinch,' as opposed to Guy Clinch in his novel. He asked for more pictures, and signed—love, Martin, with an inked X.

• • •

After sending the Amis interview to several American magazines, I wrote:

Good Friday
24 March 1988

Dear Martin,

Enclosed please find Part One of the interview we had on December 1 and 7, 1987. I sent it to *Interview* magazine in New York, and Mark Jacobson called me about it. He said he liked it, but added, "We just did Amis." I reminded him the interview was done recently and that your new novel is coming out in 1989. It would be timely to do you again as a "peg"—the term *Vanity Fair*'s editor used, as a reference for *London Fields.*

Jacobson replied, "Who is Amis's American publisher and exactly when will the book come out?" I did not know the answer so could you please tell me the date your American publisher has in mind. Jacobson implied he could find out what he had to know and he is interested in publishing the interview. I feel it would be important publicity to rev up interest in your new novel.

Meanwhile I will call you. I tried today, Good Friday, and missed you. Good luck on the final draft (you had started it when we met).

Best wishes,
Julie

• • •

During 1988 Martin and I spoke several times on the phone. He sent letters written on his Leamington Road Villas stationery, and apologized for not having written more often. His family had spent the summer in Cape Cod, and then he had flown back to New Orleans to cover the Republican Convention for *Esquire* magazine in November. The UK had a postal strike, which stopped the mail for weeks; and his new novel was in the last six months of its four-year pregnancy. He was amid the exalted—yet anxious state—of finishing, and sending it to his publisher.

His first novel, *The Rachel Papers*, was being filmed in London, but the screenplay for *Money* was still in negotiations with the studio producers wanting to put in their million dollars' worth of ten cents. He reiterated that I was not right for the young woman, Butch, nor for the older Cadutta, whose name means "falling" or "collapsed" in Italian—referring to her sagging breasts.

Martin wished he'd be sent to L.A. and he liked the photos I had sent of me sitting next to a London 'bobby' police helmet taken by a British photographer. He asked me to write and signed, love, Martin.

• • •

Seven

In August 1989 I saw Martin's life-size face on the cover of the British Edition of *GQ* at the Century City's newsstand that read, "Martin Amis: An Exclusive Extract from His New Novel." I immediately bought the British magazine and hurried home to read the excerpt "Seduction in Cold Blood," from *London Fields.* Jonathan Cape, Ltd., had just published his novel in the U.K. After eyeing every word of the sensuous chapter, I called Martin in London and said,

"Although I had suspected you of genius, now I am certain of it."

He modestly replied, "Thank you very much."

As soon as the American copies of *London Fields* hit bookstores in Los Angeles, I ran out to buy the hardcover ($19.95 plus tax) and began to read every flamboyant, Amis-ian word. I loved it. You might say I'm Martin's 'ideal reader'—as he labeled himself of Saul Bellow's. When we discussed the novel and Martin answered my questions, he told me I was a "very responsive reader," as well as "vampiric."

London Fields is a paradoxical mystery that takes place at the end of the millennium. It has well-drawn characters and settings, like the twenty-four-hour drinking club, Golgotha (Aramaic for "hill of the dead" where Christ was crucified), and the Black Cross pub where the thug, Keith

Talent and his brutish cronies and groupies hang out playing darts and pinball. These dens of iniquity are delightfully guilty pleasures to read.

Keith's main squeeze is Analiese, whom he considered "mental." (Her name clearly sounds like a preparatory ointment for sodomy.) Reading about Analiese, a chord struck me too close for comfort. For instance, Analiese sent letters to celebrities in which she "often enclosed a photograph; as a result she got replies." These photos showed her in sylvan settings perhaps with a flower. (Sounds familiar.) Her dreamy features showed "someone who could be lied to." And, after she gave herself to you…"probably wouldn't ring the house." When the dalliance was over, Analiese was left with albums, scrapbooks, memories, and letters to editors of all the tabloids. This is hilarious; Martin had (alter ego) Julienne Wells, down. (Well, not entirely.)

Keith Talent is loathsome, but in a compelling curious way. Martin created a truly despicable, dart-throwing, scalawag when he birthed Keith Talent, and actually admitted he has a soft spot for the stocky sociopath—like mothers do for their rotten, little shit kids, in spite of the evil they do.

The murderee, Nicola Six, is an alluring figure throughout the novel; nonetheless, my instincts inferred Nicola is what shrinks refer to as 'a borderline personality.' Like a sheep in wolf's clothing, Nicole comes off as a man in women's. Sometimes Nicola distinctively resembles a trannie, or transsexual. This attests to how problematic it is for a man to write from a woman's perspective; that is, to convey the internal thoughts of the feminine mind. I was not alone in my opinion. In my British hardback of *London Fields*, a female reader had penciled in the margin about Nicola's reactive, acrobatic sex: "Slick, superficial referral to sex, very masculine behavior." (Of course, a woman can perform 'acrobatic sex,' but she's probably just showing off.)

A femme fatale, Nicola Six is *überwoman:* glamorous, seductive, stylish, and intelligent—"even more than the author"—and powerful. (A skillful trans can pull off these qualities just as well—often better than many women.)

In the story, Nicola Six was also religious. She imagined "*dating God.*" "*God cried in the street outside her apartment... He wanted to marry her and have her come and live at His place.*" In drama school Nicola felt most steady playing male roles and was the lead in *Jack and the Beanstalk.* This computes that Nicola has a lot of male in her as I gleaned. Regardless of Nicola Six's XX or XY chromosomes, this female character is complex and interesting, if not always an especially believable woman.

Then there's my namesake: the foil, protagonist Guy Clinch. (Martin signed my copy, "To Julie Clinch, From the better half of me, your namesake in here, With love, Martin —1990, The Ides of March.") Guy is the ideal, but pusillanimous Mr. Nice Guy. He's rich, good looking, tall, refined, a true gentleman—in other words, effete—an ideal mark for Nicola and Keith Talent.

While engrossed in reading *London Fields*, eureka! My eyes were suddenly transfixed on the name, Walker Clinch, on page 196. I blinked and stared incredulously at the letters, W-A-L-K-E-R, realizing that Guy's father's first name differed in *one* letter from my own father's—Walter Clinch.

What's the saying? A coincidence is just a coincidence; then there are two, then three when it's no longer a coincidence. Then what is it— quantum mechanics?

• • •

The chapter on the tribulations of Guy Clinch's home and marriage describes an obsessive-compulsive household—run like a battleship and commandeered by his admiral wife, Hope. (Was she a reflection of Martin's first American wife?) Actually, the household is dominated and tyrannically ruled by his monster of an infant son, Marmaduke. The eighteen-month-old baby-Frankenstein is the most enthralling, bad-seed child conceived since Damien in *The Omen.* The chapter on changing Marmaduke's over-filled diapers will be embedded forever in my mind.

(Having a baby like Marmaduke made me want to run out and have my tubes tied.)

In the wasteland of London Fields, the good, the bad, and the ugly; the highborn and the lowlifes; the nefarious and the virtuous gravitate toward each other as they approach the event horizon of the millennium.

• • •

Eight

MARTIN AMIS COMES TO L.A.

Martin was coming to town—my town, Los Angeles, one of many cities on his American book tour schedule for his new novel, *London Fields*. An airmail envelope arrived from London, postmarked 5 March 1990, to my apartment on Cloverdale Avenue in L.A. Both the envelope and its contents were scribbled quickly by Martin's fountain pen. His note was short and to the point—he'd be in L.A. the week of March 11 for a reading and to expect his call—Love, Martin.

A male friend commented, "That's rather cocky." But I didn't find Martin's forthrightness cocky. Martin knew I'd be eager to see him. This time our meeting would be on my turf on American soil. Perhaps I would feel more personable, in the sense of a woman in the comfort of her own home.

What was I going to do? Greg and I were not together anymore. First I broke up with him, and then I started to miss him. (Or was it not having a man around?) By then, he had already found another girlfriend—rather, a matchmaking Jewish mother had found Greg, an up-and-coming L.A. artist, to be a good prospect for her single daughter. With Greg out of the picture, I looked forward to seeing Martin and having dinner with him. I didn't have an agenda for what would happen;

just getting to know him better would be enough. I'd play after dinner by ear.

Book Soup L.A

On the ides of March, March 15, 1990, Martin called to tell me he would be reading his novel, *London Fields*, at Book Soup, a popular bookstore on the Sunset Strip in West Hollywood. Earlier that day, I'd decided to wear a spaghetti-strap cocktail dress, a little number that showed a lot of skin with a hint of cleavage. After a hot shower, I sprayed Givenchy's Ysatis eau de cologne over my body, slid into the little black dress, slipped on black, silk panties and lace-topped stockings; then stepped into black, crepe de chine, Charles Jourdan stilettos with Swarovski crystals set in the heels. In fashion magazines that season I'd seen models wearing black leather, bomber jackets as evening wraps. A recent boyfriend (rebound, mistake) had left his leather jacket in my apartment. I swung it over my bare shoulders, put lipstick, compact and keys into a Chanel evening purse, and headed out.

Book Soup was only a mile from my apartment. Parking my car on a side street, I walked a block down Sunset Strip to join the crowd inside the bookstore already hanging on Martin's every word as he read pages he had bookmarked in *London Fields*. Los Angeles literati and fans filled the store, sitting on folded chairs, standing shoulder-to-shoulder, surrounding Martin as he sat on a high stool next to the front window.

Martin had chosen to read an excerpt about his pet antihero, Keith Talent—scion of the dark underbelly of London street life and champion thrower of darts at the unrepentant Black Cross pub. Martin had not yet seen me in back of the crowd where I was standing between two, high bookshelves. When he finished his reading and had answered questions from the audience, he moved to a small table in the back to sign books for the long queue that had lined up. I maneuvered among the bookshelves nearer to his signing table and he saw me. I was enchanted when Martin immediately got up from his chair and walked over to hug me, and kissed both my cheeks. We were happy to see each other and exchanged an affectionate hug.

During our embrace Martin whispered in my ear to meet him afterward in the bar at the Sofitel Hotel where he was staying in Beverly Hills. He said we'd have dinner in the hotel's French restaurant. Martin had a ride provided by his publisher, so I agreed to drive to the hotel and meet him in the lounge.

Our brief conversation at Book Soup attracted the attention of many people waiting for Martin to sign their books. As soon as Martin returned to the signing table, I started for the door and a stylish L.A. woman came up to me and asked, "Are you friends with Martin?"

I was taken aback by her sudden approach and obvious delight that I knew the famous British author. Los Angelinos usually don't acknowledge celebrities or actors because we see them all the time, shopping, driving their luxury cars, stepping out of limos, and going about their business. The woman was attractive and smartly dressed with an air of old Los Angeles money.

Visiting Martin Amis

I quickly replied, "He's married!" as if to defend Martin's honor, and not mine. I don't know why I reacted so defensively, considering the woman had merely asked an innocent question—not implying that I knew him intimately. I wish I had been more gracious. The downfall of my nerves!

I drove to the Sofitel Hotel, again parking my Japanese car on the street, not with the hotel valet. I blended in Beverly Hills in dress and composure as my designer heels clicked-clacked up the white granite stairs to the hotel entrance and the doorman politely greeted me. Thanking him, I went straight into the bar, sat down, and ordered a drink. I remember going to AA meetings at the time (these were episodic, depending on the month and the year) so more than likely, I ordered a Diet Coke. Soon, Martin arrived, and again kissed me on both cheeks. He sat down and ordered a French imported cabernet from the French waiter. We immediately began a lively conversation after our long anticipation of meeting again.

We talked about our lives, what we'd been doing. Martin mentioned his sister, Sally, had been having a terrible time recently. She had come home to find her boyfriend dead on the floor of her flat, and was recovering from the trauma. (He didn't say what had caused his death.)

"My sister is a fabulous alcoholic," Martin added.

"Well," I said, "I'm an un-fabulous one."

Martin laughed.

Sadly, several years later, Sally Amis, passed away at age 46.

Martin wanted to know what it was like living in Los Angeles. He had visited L.A. before, and stayed at the Beverly Wilshire Hotel while hired to co-script the screenplay for *Saturn 3* with Farrah Fawcett and Kirk Douglas. Since we had last seen each other, Martin had seen *Barfly*, the film based on L.A. poet and author, Charles Bukowski, starring Mickey Rourke and Faye Dunaway. He said the Los Angeles depicted in the film was unreal to him.

"Of course, it is," I said. "That's because *Barfly* was filmed in the seedy downtown section of L.A. where Bukowski, an unapologetic drunk, lived among L.A.'s down-and-out denizens in cheap bars and rundown, old apartment buildings, and the mentally ill, homeless and winos roamed the streets." I indicated with my glass toward the Sofitel's affluent ambiance, "Around here, everyone is rich or famous. It's anonymous people like me who are unique. We are the elite—a special minority. "

Martin's eyelid muscles strained, eyes focused, pupils rigid, noting: "That's an interesting concept." I envisioned the cartoon caption above his head and teased, "You aren't going to write a story about that, are you?" He merely smiled, tucking the notion away in a file in his hippo-campus. $^\Omega$

Martin went on to wax delight about *Barfly*. He recounted the scene in the seedy bar when the bartender, played by Sylvester Stallone's brother, Frank, shouted at a drunk across the counter,

"Your mother's c**t smells like carpet cleaner!"

I instantly cringed—then chastised Martin for repeating the vulgar line. "I had a feeling you were going to say that!" I said, as I took a sip of my Diet Coke. Now I wished it had my favorite French bird, Gray Goose, in it.

Afterwards we moved into the hotel dining room and were seated at a linen covered table, Martin ordered a steak and another glass of wine. Whenever we had dinner, Martin would order the choice cut of beef on the menu, and I had the catch-of-the-day; tonight it was butter-grilled, white fish.

Our French waiter was jovial and "extra friendly,"—as Ed Ruscha had once described a jolly, art collector. The waiter spoke with a thick, French accent that prompted Martin to remark that it wasn't real.

"His accent is fake. He's putting on a French accent," Martin sur-mised the waiter was playing up the hotel's Gallic atmosphere.

Ω A few years later, Martin wrote a short story titled "Straight Fiction" for Esquire (Dec.1995) in which, demographically, being gay ('gaynicity') was the norm. In it, homosexuality was the majority sexual preference in society. If you had the misfortune of being heterosexual, it was not only 'not cool,' but also hazardous. As it were, 'hetero-bashing' was a popular pastime by homosexual thugs in this new, hip, modern world. Ironically, within a decade of the fiction, millennials accepted being gay as an alternative life style, and homosexuals no longer had to hide in the closet.)

"I think his accent is authentic. He's a Frenchman speaking English."

Martin disagreed. "It sounds phony to me. It's obviously affected."

We decided to settle the matter by asking the waiter if he were really French or an actor pretending to be. Marcel (he introduced himself) assured us he was, indeed, a bona fide Frenchman: "*Mai oui, c'est verité. Je suis français.*"

Martin remained dubious. He just didn't believe him. "Let's test him. When he comes back, I'll ask him a word only a Frenchman would know."

When Marcel returned with the escargots, Martin posed the French word to him. "What does *dégueulasse* mean?"

Marcel quickly replied, "Eet eez zumzing zat is ter-ree-blay des-scooz-teeng!"

Finally, Martin gave in— Marcel might really be French, but I discerned he remained skeptical.

I gave him the point, "Well, this is Hollywood, and every other waiter is an actor, so it's only reasonable to think he's acting."

Living in this town—even for me—was often difficult to "separate the chicken shit from the chicken salad" —as the great Dean Martin used to say.

N.B.: Years later, I told the phony French accent story to the front desk clerk at the Sofitel Hotel in Philadelphia. The Frenchman verified that the meaning of the French word was, indeed, offensive and vulgar. He said the French connotation of *dégueulasse* was almost like saying "f*cking disgusting."

During dinner Martin told me about his American book tour, the cities he'd been to, and how pleased he was that his American readers enthusiastically received him and his novels. Martin reciprocated their affection and he was delighted that *London Fields* made the New York Times bestseller list—as had his dark novel about America, *Money: A Suicide Note*. Martin definitely loved America and its energetic zeitgeist. It's no wonder he eventually moved to live here.

I recanted my naïveté during the previous interview about not having social classes in America as in England. "You don't see any homeless people in here, do you?"

Martin looked around, and nodded; but we both agreed the class system in America was not like it was in England. Here, it has always been based on money.

Martin signed the bill to the room on his expense account. We walked through the lobby to the elevator and we walked silently to his room. As Martin opened the door we entered a plush, Parisian decored suite. The ambience was Old World, darkened by burnt umber walls and high ceiling. A French provincial armoire stood against the wall. Heavy, burgundy drapes covered the floor-to-ceiling windows and a mahogany sleigh bed filled most of the room.

Breaking the tension, I sat down on a chair, balanced my elbow on a small table, and challenged Martin to an arm-wrestling match. He immediately took up my offer, and sat down on the opposite chair and propped his right elbow next to mine. Both of us gave our best effort to collapse the other's arm and declare him or herself winner. The game was a simple act of dominance. Unconsciously, there's always a vying of power between a couple in a relationship as to who has the upper hand (psychologically speaking.)

In a relationship it's not a matter of physical strength. Instead, like in guerilla warfare, it's how one uses strategy—in combination with skill and tactical prowess—that will determine who will take control. Dominance can change over time, but the dynamics of the game will continue until one reconciles or surrenders to who ultimately controls the relationship, or bows out.

Of course, Martin won. In less than ten seconds he flipped my forearm down flat on the table. This was not done without diligent effort on his part because I had been working out for months at the Hollywood YMCA, getting in shape—if not exactly for this physical takedown.

After congratulating Martin on his victory, I gave him the due masculine respect and admiration that Black Cross darts groupie, Trish

Visiting Martin Amis

Stewart, gave Keith Talent in *London Fields*. Martin and I had fun playing like kids in the privacy of the room. I took off one of my Dior crescent diamond earrings and clasped it on Martin's earlobe, commenting how exotic it looked on him. I told him to see for himself in the long mirror inside the armoire door. It's fortunate Martin's comfortable in his male skin in today's world when people can decide which sex they are; he'd make a very masculine transvestite, 'a sheep in wolf's clothing.'

Finally relaxed after a long day, Martin took off his jacket and hung it over a chair. I'm no fashion guru and admit my sartorial style has not been without my share of outlandish outfits; but I noticed Martin seemed quite fond of a tyrannosaurus shade of green in a lightweight suit I saw him wear on more than one occasion. The asparagus hue of this particular verdant carapace would have looked better on an amphibian—underwater. Did he really go into a men's clothing store, point to the Jurassic-green suit on the rack, and say, "I'll take it?" (Perhaps its light, no-iron fabric, was practical to wear on book tours…)

Seeing my copy of *London Fields* placed on the bed, Martin asked,
"Don't you want me to sign it?"
Not a big autograph hound, I said, "Sure, if you want to."
"What do you want me to write?"
"To Julie, the greatest sex I ever had."
We both laughed at my off-the-wall suggestion.
He signed the title page, "To Julie Clinch, from the better half of me, your namesake, in here, —with love, Martin. 1990, the Ides of March."

We enjoyed more repartee until it was time for me to leave. Only an expert in the art on osculation could have written "The Concordance of Nicola Six's Kisses," in *London Fields*. [7] Martin had to catch a plane to San Francisco in the morning, his next stop on the book tour.

---

7 Martin Amis, *London Fields*. "The Concordance of Nicola Six's Kisses." London: Jonathan Cape, Ltd., (1989) Chapter 11, p.186.

After a long day Martin got into bed, and I tucked him in and whispered, "Good night, sweet prince." His face glowed in the dim light of the room at the sound of Juliet's farewell to Romeo. I turned off the small lamp and silently left the room.

• • •

Nine

A letter from Martin arrived after our dinner at the Sofitel Hotel. The date on London postmark stamp was blurred, but it was shortly after Martin returned from his American book tour.

Martin thanked me for my letter. He added that he especially like my last query about the miscreant, Keith Talent, in *London Fields*. He said it was a nice change from literary pundits who ask him questions like: "How do you reconcile reality and myth in the satirical text?"

Martin answered my question directly. "No, Nicola did not give Keith a blowjob in the men's room before the darts tournament. Keith's girl-friend, Trish, thinks she does but Nicola only knelt down to straighten Keith's trousers to build his male confidence by female submission." Martin admitted he made the scene a little ambiguous on purpose and complemented me that I was a "responsible reader."

Martin said he'd recovered from his American tour—Los Angeles had been its highlight and that he'd never forget it. Martin brought up the arm-wrestling we did in the room and continued at a recent dinner party in London, challenging anyone who dared to pin down his arm. He 'took on all comers, one fist after the other came down on the table.'

He jokingly claimed arms all over town hung in slings the next day. He said I had given more trouble than most of the men at the party.

On the last leg of his tour, he had stopped in Minneapolis, finding time to shoot some pool, but it was a letdown after L.A. His final reading was in Chicago where he had time to catch up on his sleep for a few nights before the long flight back to England.

He asked me to write soon and send photos.

• • •

A letter postmarked 23 July 1990 from Great Britain to Los Angeles was written on Martin's writing flat letterhead.

Martin said to wait until he returned from Cape Cod before sending photographs. He spent his summer holiday with his wife's family every August. He enjoyed playing with his boys on the sandy beach in New England, but it was stressful flying across the Atlantic Ocean with two young children. "Rolling, rolling, rolling..." (1970s TV series, *Wagon Train.*)

I had previously written notes addressed to two of the main characters in *London Fields*, Keith Talent and Guy Clinch, in my last letter, and the imaginary men thanked me. (The antagonist, bad boy "Keith was especially keen" about my message.)

Martin admitted the subject of his body of work and that of his father was complicated and deep. This seems natural, considering a relationship between a father and son is always complex and influences life. Martin had dedicated *London Fields* to his dad, Kingsley, and admitted he had borrowed a lot from his father's novels. He was relieved that they had both come to terms with issues concerning his older brother.

Martin answered the question my friend, Pamela, had asked: Where had he gotten the name for Sheriff Groves in his short story, "Insight at Flame Lake"? Martin explained it was from General Leslie Groves, the U.S. Army General, who was in charge of the Manhattan Project, the U.S. Army Corps production of the atomic bomb.

Visiting Martin Amis

Again Martin flattered my 'vampiric' reading and that he'd write in September—signed, with love.

• • •

A handwritten envelope to Julie Clinch, Cloverdale Ave., L.A., CA., posted 7 December 1990, Paddington, Great Britain, arrived in my mailbox.

The envelope contained a letter and a black and white photograph of young Martin Amis standing on a tree-lined road in France. He captioned the photo of him was taken in Paris at age twenty-five, and that "even then you could still look like shit." I disagree. Martin is very photogenic —good-looking. The slightly dour expression on his youthful face was seductive.

Martin apologized for not writing in a while. A lot had happened since he had last written and his summer had turned into a flurry of deadlines and drama. He questioned how he had escaped the problems that afflicted his two siblings, and concluded his writing was great therapy and had saved him from being prescribed lithium with Nurse Ratchet to dole them out (that is my metaphor.) He was glad to report his older brother—by one year—was doing much better.

Also he had been going back and forth to Paris for a family in-law who was ill. It was in Paris that he had written *Other People* and that he had always thought of The City of Light as a good time—going to bars and pinball, art museums, etc., so it was depressing to go at a bad time.

My letter had arrived after he started writing me. He was sorry he was such a bad pen pal, but told me writers are not good at it because that's what they do all day. Martin wondered how those "chubby Victorians" did it so often? Now we can telephone or Fax. (Note: A few years after this letter, Silicon Valley would make a paradigm leap in technology in communication: emails, cell phones, texting, Instagram, etc.) He asked me to write back, and not to be down— that we both were at a difficult age. Then reflected, what age isn't difficult? Martin told me that I had a beautiful body and was great company. [Thank you very much, so are you. As far as company goes, you don't find much better than his.] Again, he signed, love, Mart. (I suspect he signed most of his personal letters to women with this salutation. Nevertheless, I was flattered.)

Martin in Paris at age 25

• • •

Ten

The Background, Europe and Morocco

"I say all this because I am part of the story I am going to tell, and I feel the need to give some idea of where I'm coming from."

—*Mike Hooligan, Night Train* Martin Amis [8]

Again, I was living L.A., "The City of Angels," "La La Land," "Hollyweird," "Tinsel Town," the "Land of Broken Dreams," whatever you want to call it. I left Los Angeles after I graduated from UCLA; now I'd come back. This time I was determined to stay and find work in the film industry. Like most actors who not yet 'made it' in Hollywood, we strived to make ends meet as we experienced the mercurial highs and heart aching lows of young emotions. We went on countless auditions for film or TV work; sometimes we got the part, but most of the time we didn't. Professional rejections, plus those from a lover were hard to endure, but life goes on. We enjoyed our days in the sun along with our common tales of woe. First, though, I want to reflect on what happened during the two years before I returned to Los Angeles.

---

8 Martin Amis, *Night Train*. New York: Harmony Books. (1998) p.14

With a bachelor's degree, my first professional job was as a social worker for the Department of Aid to Families with Dependent Children for Los Angeles County. This venture brought me on the Road to Damascus when I realized the virtues of socialism that was inculcated in public school system wasn't all it was cracked up to be in the real world. In my sixty-family caseload, a notable number of public-dependent families who were allocated monthly welfare checks, housing, and other benefits seemed to be happier than I was; at least, they had each other to share life with. After an eight-hour day at work, I drove home on a backed-up freeway, exhausted to a lonely bedroom I had rented from a crazy woman next to the UCLA campus, and slept in a little cot she had jimmied up in her garden apartment.

Within a few months I suffered job burnout from social work. Looking back, it was more a culture shock after hitting raw reality head-on in the streets of downtown L.A. Nineteenth century philosopher, John Stuart Mills called his nervous breakdown a "culture crisis" after he graduated from college in England. I shared his emotional crisis, but not his intellect.

When reality dashed my illusions of what I imagined life would be like after college, I plummeted into a deep depression. I sold my old Volvo car, packed up what little belongings I had, and flew back to my mother's home in Washington State.

Seeing my emotional collapse, my mom wondered if sending me to college had been a mistake, even though it had been the goal for middle class parents across America who had grown up in the Great Depression.

In an attempt to get me out of my comatose existence in which I had succumbed in my high school bedroom, Mother opted to send me to Europe and bought a plane ticket for me to London. She gave me two hundred dollars worth of travelers' checks to make my way through Europe. A cousin my age, Sherry, wanted to join me on my overseas journey and we flew to London out of Vancouver, B.C.

Once Sherry and I recovered from jetlag with a good night's sleep in a London hotel, we hit the friendly streets and met a lot of people in their early twenties like us who were eager to mingle with young Americans. In the 1960s, English boys were labeled either "mods" or "teddy boys," according to their distinctive life style and dress. Running around London during the day, we slept at night in youth hostels for a few English pounds. After a week of British adventure and revelry, we hitchhiked to Dover on the east coast to cross the English Channel by boat to Calais, France, where we continued to hitchhike down to Paris, and again checked into youth hostels. In the mornings we watched French girls standing at communal bathroom, soaping their private parts as we brushed our teeth. We took showers.

Napoleon tomb, Paris

Biarritz, France

Continuing the tour of France we hitchhiked south to the coastal city of Bordeaux, greeted by its refreshing sea air and friendly citizens.

French people invited us to their family homes for dinner or drove us to further destinations. A Frenchman flew us in his private propeller plane to the fancy resort town of Biarritz. We always found a youth hostel in towns we passed through for inexpensive but clean lodgings. We continued to hitchhike thorough the Pyrenees Mountains down to Madrid—meeting both Basque and Spanish people—going along wherever adventure our road led us.

The festive city of Madrid was crowded with Latin citizens and hucksters in its colorful streets; Spaniards and foreigners were busying around us. Peripatetic gypsies and their children circled, asking for our hand to give a reading into our future, always demanding more pesetas.

My main priority was to visit the magnificent Prado Museum. Filled with masterpieces of the royal palace painters, Goya, Velasquez, and El Greco (the Greek), its walls were hung with other great European masters. The Prado was my favorite treasure trove in all of Spain.

At the time a political change was fomenting in the Spanish air because old President Franco was expected to soon die, and the present ad hoc government was on alert for potential civil rebellion. When I danced with a Spanish man in civilian clothes at a public square fiesta, I felt the revolver in his holster press upon my waist while we waltzed to the outdoor music.

For an excursion, Sherry and I boarded a train to Lisbon, Portugal. We shared a cabin with a young America couple, and sat across from two large, Spanish army officers. One was reading a Spanish newspaper that had photos of the American antiwar movement against the Vietnam War and shots of college student protests. The corpulent officer—a shoo-in for Poncho Villa with bandoliers of bullet cartridges crisscrossed over his huge chest—boasted, "*Mucho paz in España,*" as he padded the revolver holstered on his wide waist. The American girl translated his caveat: "Much peace in Spain." They didn't put up with that nonsense.

Returning to Spain, we made our way down back-traveled roads to Seville and walked through the majestic, centuries old Alcázar Royal Palace, then on to the grand Alhambra Palace in Granada. Both Muslim palaces were designed in medieval, Islamic *mudéjar* architecture for the Moorish Caliphates of Castile and Andalusia (Al-Andalus) in the Middle Ages when the Moors ruled from 711 to 1492. Many Muslims converted (*conversos*) and remained in the Iberian land after the Christian *Reconquista* in 1492 when Queen Isabella and King Ferdinand conquered the Moors and confiscated their magnificent palaces to reign over Spain. The Catholic royal couple usurped the Great Mosque of Cordoba, the seat of the Mohammad Caliphate of Spain from which the Moors ruled Spain for 800 years during its Golden Age.

Me in front of Alcazar Royal Palace, Seville

Part of the 5th season of "Game of Thrones" was shot in several locations in Seville, including the Alcázar Royal Palace.

Alhambra, Granada, Spain

• • •

Sherry and I hitchhiked to Costa del Sol on the Spanish southern coastline to board a ferry to cross the Mediterranean Sea. We passed by the

Rock of Gibraltar (named by Al Tar, the Moor who claimed it) as we headed toward the seaport of Tangiers on the northern tip of North Africa. By now our fellow passengers were mostly Arabs and Moroccans, dressed in native *dishdashas* (long, Arab tunics). My only past exposure to Arabs was virtually from the film, *Casablanca*, starring Humphrey Bogart and Ingrid Bergman, so my naïve xenophobia imagined all Middle Eastern men had *khanjab* daggers hidden beneath their robes ready to pull out at any moment. The stereotype changed after we met three young, Moroccans who changed my prejudice with their delightful and disarming personalities. The dark complexioned youths were students from university in London, returning to their hometowns in Morocco. Fashionably dressed in English clothing, the young men introduced themselves and had us charmed within five minutes. Everyone enjoyed the lively conversation onboard the boat to North Africa.

Moroccan young men

Upon landing in Tangiers, we traveled on the bus with the Ali, Mohammad, and Jubal to Rabat, the capital of Morocco. Getting to know the boys better on the bus, one of them, Ali invited Sherry and me to meet his family in Rabat. When we reached his hometown, we accepted Ali's invitation to dinner. I remember the warm hospitality with which Ali's family welcomed us into their traditional Arab home. His mother and sisters had prepared a sumptuous supper of traditional Moroccan cuisine: couscous with vegetables and lamb, *Kefta Mkawra*, a main dish of spicy beef meatballs and tomato tagging, and pita bread. We sat on pillows on the floor around a low table and enjoyed listening to the family's conversation in Arabic that Ali translated for us. We washed our hands in offered water bowls and shared the delicious plates of food and pita bread, using our right hand (the left hand is verboten due to cultural taboos) into the communal dishes on the table.

After the two-hour dinner we thanked Ali and his mother and sisters for cooking the delicious meal and for their lovely hospitality. We found a small, nearby hotel in Rabat to spend the night. Early the next morning Sherry and I boarded a sturdy old bus for the long ride south to Casablanca.

Casablanca

Casablanca taxi

The French-Moroccan city of Casablanca was everything I imagined an old Middle-Eastern city would be like in the twentieth century. Sherry and I walked the entire day through the bustling outdoor markets in the *casbah* where I bought a fringed, goatskin handbag and Arabic, polished stone bracelets. Old men sat on the dirt street against centuries-old buildings selling claw-bound, live chickens. We looked for Bogart's bar, "Rick's Café" from the eponymous film to no avail.

After we explored the maze-like alleyways in the Old Medina—the ancient quarter of Casablanca—we needed a good night's sleep and checked into a small hotel for a few dirham. In the morning we embarked again on a rickety old bus filled with Moroccans and their chickens and goats for the dusty, three-hour ride inland to the magical city of Marrakech.

Marrakech is an exotic, magnificent city oasis in the North Sahara Desert, populated with modern and traditional Moroccan citizens. We strolled on stone streets of the *casbah* and watched young male entertainers on street corners with tins for donations, and then walked through open-air markets, unchanged for centuries. Old women sat on blankets on dirt streets selling homemade pita bread. A bevy of local merchants sold their wares and open-cooked lamb shish kabob. Aromatic spices in reds, orange, and gold were packed in large, open barrels; bins of dried fruits, dates and nuts; leather jackets, purses and sandals hung from hooks; handcrafted bronze and polished stone bracelets and jewelry were displayed for bargain prices.

Snake charmer in Marrakech

Visiting Martin Amis

Marrakech woman selling bread

Young and ingenuous, Sherry and I wore short skirts in the Western style, our long hair uncovered as we walked through the tall, tangerine-red painted gates into the Red City, the ancient *medina* in Marrakech. We explored the original Arab quarter through its narrow, stone streets and open-air markets—as they have been for a thousand years. In the town square, snake charmers tempted cobras out of weaved baskets for the mesmerized crowd. We walked over to pet the camels and donkeys standing in the shade while the nearby owners curiously eyed us. Only Donkeys and camels can be used for transport inside the Red City walls.

We continued to explore the Red City's medieval alleyways between high, white stucco buildings, never encountering a disapproving look, nor accosted by an insult or gesture as we had been on the streets of southern Spain. (In Seville, a young boy poked his hand up my dress as policemen on the corner laughed at my scream.) Surely, Muslims viewed our Western dress as immodest, but European and Americans had often come to their former French colonial country; Moroccans treated us kindly in spite of our *dhimmis* (non-Muslim) status. This was twenty years before radical *mujahideen* (militant Islamists) Al Qaeda, and later, the savage ISIS, had declared jihad against the West. These Islamists proclaimed a holy war against all infidels and religions—including other Muslims—that did not conform to their extreme form of Islam fundamentalism.

During our time in Morocco, we did not witness hostility against Westerners or us. In fact, Moroccans were invariably hospitable and we enjoyed visiting their peaceful country. Nevertheless, I was relieved to return to Spain and feel the familiar ground of Western civilization beneath my feet. Although southern Spain still had vestiges of Moorish influence, I felt at home again on Occidental soil. People are more naturally more comfortable in their own culture—Middle Easterners in Islamic lands, and Westerners in their familiar Judeo-Christian. Metaphorically, we like to be in own sandbox.

• • •

When we hitchhiked back to Costa del Sol, Sherry wanted to take another boat ride, this time to the tourist island of Ibiza. By then I had met a Spanish boy on the beach in Almèria and decided to stay with him at a friendly Spanish family's camping site and pool grounds that had delicious Spanish *paella*—a delicious casserole of *mariscos,* shrimp, mussels, and chicken in saffron rice, and *sangria,* fresh fruit mixed in red wine to wash it down.

When Sherry left for the Spanish island, Ibiza, I told her I'd meet her there in a week. Thanks to my Spanish conquistador, Julio, I never made it.

One day at the pool where Julio and I were staying, I heard that an Italian and French film productions were filming in locations in the nearby hills. The landscape and desert terrain outside Almèria on the southern coast of Spain resembles the American southwest with rolling hills, red cliffs, sagebrush, and wide plateaus. Westerns and desert battle scenes have been filmed here since the 1940s, '50s, and '60s, (*El Cid* with Charlton Heston). Italian director, Sergio Leone made his "spaghetti westerns," here; e.g., *The Good, The Bad, and The Ugly*, and two sequels starring Clint Eastwood became international blockbusters around the world. Western movies are often shot in the ideal cowboys and Indians topology with Spanish locals hired to play Mexicans for ten dollars a day to stand around in the blazing sun. I was hired in a French "Western" to pose as a town lady in the Old West.

One hot, dusty afternoon I wandered over a rocky hill to visit another film set. The movie was part of Sergio Leone's Mexican Revolution trilogy that took place in 1913 Mexico.

Western film in Almèria, Spain

When the pudgy, lead actor heard my American accent, he approached me and curiously inquired, "What are you doing here in Spain?"

"I came to Europe to find myself," I said, peering into at his murky, brown eyes.

Looking back, I probably learned the metaphysical jargon from an existential course I took in the UCLA philosophy department. I wasn't even sure what I meant but used it as an abstract concept for searching what to do with my life. In any case, it piqued the actor's interest, and he invited me to dinner that night at his beachfront hotel, a modern high-rise on the Costa del Sol shoreline that had a panoramic view of the Mediterranean Sea. That evening when we were dining in the hotel restaurant, I watched James Coburn sitting alone at a nearby table while the actor facing me pontificated nonstop about himself as he drank Spanish wine from two bottles he'd ordered. I remember wishing I were sitting across from Coburn instead of him.

After we finished dinner, the actor persuaded me to accompany him to his penthouse suite in the hotel. I soon came to regret it. His large suite took up half the top floor, next to another penthouse, presumably Coburn's. I could see the top of the Rock of Gibraltar glistening in the moonlight from the wide balcony overlooking the Mediterranean Sea, and farther away make out a dim outline of what may have been Algiers or Tangiers on the southern horizon.

I didn't know yet that a woman does not go into an alpha male's hotel room unless it is implicitly understood that consensual sex is expected. The very act of a woman entering a private room with a man alone will imply sex in the mind of an alpha man—it certainly was not in mine. My limited dating experience had been with boys in high school, and more recently, immature frat boys at university who drank too much and were party animals—but not rapists—at least, not at the time in my experience.

This actor proceeded to drink more liquor in the suite, constantly pouring brandy into his glass before it was empty. He continuously walked around in a circle as if he were onstage, a simulacrum of an overweight, balding Hamlet reciting a monologue as he became more and more intoxicated. Except this actor was not reciting Hamlet's famous "To be or not to be" soliloquy—it was more like, 'To be *me*, or not to be *me*!' He went on to boast what a great actor he was—how he had married "the most beautiful woman in the world;" that every film critic didn't appreciate him as the most talented actor of his day, and so on. By this time, I was getting quite bored by his drunken screed and one-man show, and had had enough of his Globe Theater stage show, starring him. So I announced it was time for me to go home. To my surprise, the pudgy, drunk Hamlet freaked.

"What? You can't leave!" he exclaimed. "You don't go to a man's hotel room and then leave!"

"What do you expect me to do? Stay here all night?" I asked.

"Stay with me, of course. What did you think when you came up here with me?" he demanded.

"I didn't think anything, but I wasn't going to go to bed with you. I don't even know you!"

Infuriated, he yelled, "Don't know me? Everyone knows me! I won the Academy Award! I'm famous around the world!"

"Just because I can see you for twenty-five cents at a matinee in a corner movie theater doesn't mean I know you!" I snapped back.

Hearing my impudent retort, the actor quickly crossed the room to me standing with my purse prepared to leave, and lifted me up against the wall next to the open balcony overlooking the sea below. Watching the moonlight reflect on the dancing waves, I felt I would soon be floundering in them. He held me on the wall for a moment, and then released me, realizing he had come close to throwing me over the balcony.

Needless to say, I was quite shaken; I literally thought he was going to toss me off the balcony into the sea. I instinctively went into survival mode, complying with this drunken madman's demands. (The term, 'date rape' had not yet been coined to describe sexual assault after a dinner date and movie.)

In the morning the actor arrogantly told me, "I could use a girl like you," after he had sexually assaulted me. I felt abused and humiliated. All I knew was I wanted to get away from him as soon as I could. After he left the hotel to go to work on the film, I slipped away...and never looked back.

My adventures traveling from England and France to Spain and Portugal, through Morocco in North Africa, then back to Spain, up to Switzerland, and back to Paris—grounded me. I felt fully recovered from the existential crisis I had suffered after university. Motivated, I decided to resume my inchoate life back in the United States, and flew back to America. I wrote a check at the Paris airline counter because I didn't have any money to buy a plane ticket. The first thing I did when I returned to my hometown was to deposit money in my bank account so the check wouldn't bounce.

Eleven

HOLLYWOODLAND

Who would want the socialist Utopia?
Especially if you were at all artistic –
you want all those inequalities, because
that's what makes life interesting.

— MARTIN AMIS

After a year traveling in Europe and North Africa, I enrolled at Cal State College to get a California teaching credential in secondary education. That completed, I taught in a junior high school for a year in the San Francisco Bay area. It seemed my life had come to a stalemate; so during the summer I decided to move back to Los Angeles.

Driving south, down the Pacific Coast Highway in my 1967 Mustang Fastback ('four on the floor' stick shift, eight cylinder, 289 CI), I had decided to pursue an acting career. This wasn't a very original pursuit for a young woman in Hollywood, but my decision to work in the film industry wasn't far-fetched since I had acted in high school plays and local theaters. I had also taken acting classes in the UCLA Theater Arts department and had attended its summer acting workshop. In my senior year, I'd won the Theater Arts department's best actress award.

When I graduated from college, I thought a career in acting was somewhat frivolous. Besides, I'd heard stories about the casting couch and how hard it was for a woman in the ruthless world of show business. But then, a good job anywhere, at least for women at the time, sometimes required pleasing your boss for job security. It was very much a man's world. It happened in most work places. If that were the case, I'd trade a pass in the teachers' lounge for one on the casting couch. As my mom used to say, "You can't blame a dog for trying." Those were the good old days for men, but not for women. We didn't have much recourse but to grin and bear sexual harassment, or leave the job and find another that didn't demand your integrity. Thanks to brave women for speaking up, nowadays is a much better world for women in the workplace.

In the first week I returned to L.A., I joined the Screen Actors Guild, thanks to my former drama teacher, Professor John Cauble, at UCLA Theater Arts, who had heard of a SAG film production currently shooting in Venice Beach. I auditioned and got the part of a college girl whom the lead actor, Richard Hatch, tries to pick up in a beach bar. The S.A.G. acting job enabled me to register as a member of Screen Actors Guild on Sunset Boulevard. With a union card, I signed with a theatrical agent in Hollywood who sent me on more film auditions.

After settling into an apartment in West Hollywood, I read a casting call for a major film, *Missouri Breaks,* in *Variety* (Hollywood trade paper) was in preproduction at Sam Goldwyn Studios, and had a call for American Indians. (The PC term, Native American, had not yet been mandated). I telephoned the studio and asked for the production office.

A male voice answered, "Jack Nicholson speaking."

"Hello, Mr. Nicholson. I read you're looking for Indians to audition for your movie. I have Mohican blood and would like to come in to audition."

"The office is closed now, so call tomorrow and ask for the casting director," Jack said.

"Well, you're there now and I live very close."

"I'm leaving soon, so call tomorrow."

"I could be there in fifteen minutes. I think it would be worth your while." I gave it my best shot and it worked.

There was a pause and Jack said. "Fifteen minutes."

I quickly dressed in a white shirt and taupe skirt, and then drove to Goldwyn Studios, past the guard gate where Jack had left a pass for me.

I entered an old office with hardwood floors and drably painted walls to see Jack Nicholson sitting behind a large, oak desk. I sat in a chair facing him. After introductions, he stared me down in his best 'I have the power' look. I stared back, not blinking, into his Absinthe-green eyes.

After a minute of stare down, Jack said, "You don't look very Indian to me,"

"Well, I am. My father told me there was Mohican blood on his side." (My Aunt Mary, his sister in Saint Louis, later told me that my dad was known to embellish, if not outright fabricate, stories like this.)

"Leave a resume and photo, and I'll give it to the casting agent."

"Thank you for seeing me." And I turned and left the building.

Looking back, I don't know where I got the unmitigated gall to do this kind of thing, but I've heard many actors do these outlandish stunts—anything to get in the door. I never heard from the casting director—but he did cast Marlon Brando as one of the leads.

I managed to get into some doors, but it was through my theatrical agency. I auditioned and got acting roles on TV in *The Blue Knight* with George Kennedy, and *The Bob Newhart Show*. I played the floozy girl friend of a Texan in the film, *Assault on Paradise* starring Oliver Reed, which was filmed on location in Phoenix, Arizona. (The film was released as *The Maniac* because another film already had the original title.) I remember Oliver Reed and Robert Mitchum's son, Jim, arrived on the desert set at 7:00 a.m., unshaven and disheveled, their eyes reddened and blurry from partying all night.

I got roles in other 1970s TV series; a memorable scene with Robert Wagner, in which I played a Vegas showgirl in the series, *Hart to Hart*, and in *McMillan and Wife* with Rock Hudson. I was twice cast in parts in the popular L.A. cop series, *Starsky and Hutch*. The sound-man told me that David Soul, who played Hutch, would have to redo several takes by the end of the day, having drunk many beers between the afternoon scenes shootings.

Alcohol has always been a staple in film production and flowed freely after the AD yelled, "That's a wrap," at the end of a shoot or when a film or TV season was over. But a distinct hard drug surfaced out of the streets and into the mainstream in the 1970s, and became the drug of choice in the film industry.

By the early eighties, cocaine was as ubiquitous in the film industry as sex harassment. "Coke" had become particularly popular at parties and in nightclubs, restaurants, and inside movie studios. The stimulant effects of cocaine made it the preferred drug on all levels of the movie business from the blue-collar crews, grips and technicians; to actors, directors, and producers; and "the suits," executives in the Tower.

Starsky & Hutch role

• • •

S till in my twenties, and said to be *jolie*, I was invited to a lot of Hollywood parties—one in which I met Peter Lawford who was reclining on a bed in the Hollywood apartment of actress Connie Sellecca for a someone's engagement celebration.

Lawford asked me if I had ever had "this," and pointed to a small glass vial in his hand filled with white powder. When I told him 'no,' he scooped out a dollop with a small, silver spoon on a gold chain hanging from his neck. It was cocaine. Peter told me to sniff the powder in a nostril from the spoon and hold it in my lungs. I did, but I didn't feel anything. Years later, I felt something, but that's another chapter. In my opinion, it's a very overrated drug.

I continued going on auditions for film work and got small roles in TV soap operas, *Days of our Lives* and *General Hospital*. I was introduced to producer Bill Orr, who had been married to Jack Warner's daughter and was head of Warner Brothers Television, which had big hits like *Maverick* starring James Garner. One time I went to dinner with Milos Foreman who was directing *One Flew Over the Cuckoo's Nest*, for which he would win the Oscar for best director. Milos Forman was a gentleman. But other directors weren't and I wasn't the type to go down the well-worn path of trading my body for a part in a movie. It wasn't easy to keep a moral compass and making ends meet in a world of situational ethics. Like any actor in the world Hollywood, I experienced the agony and the ecstasy of show business.

For the next few years I managed to pay my rent on the first of the month for my West Hollywood, one-bedroom apartment on North Poinsettia Place, by earning a living during the day by substitute teaching and acting jobs. I kept an active social life on the weekend.

Networking at clubs and actors' bar hangouts in West Hollywood, a friend told me to try out for the theatrical stage production of *The Hostage*, a play by Irish playwright, Brendan Behan that was being cast in a small Hollywood theater. I landed the part of Nicole, the Irish prostitute with the proverbial heart of gold. James Cromwell, son of the famous director, John Cromwell, played the role of the British hostage.

Drinking Guinness with the cast members after the curtain went down, I enjoyed the fellowship of other actors in the play who were struggling to make it in Hollywood. (James went on to a successful film career from his early role in *Death by Murder*—with a celebrity cast of Alec Guinness, Maggie Smith, Peter Sellers, and Truman Capote. Later, James played the farmer in the blockbuster film, *Babe*, about a sheepherding piglet. Continuing his career, James was the chauffeur in the Oscar's best picture, *The Artist*.

After seven months of six evening performances a week plus two matinees, *The Hostage* closed. With the abrupt end of a busy acting role, I was depressed and self-medicated with red wine or an occasional, bifurcated Quaalude…when I could score one. (We gave a Mona Lisa-smile when referring to "a half," meaning half a 'lude.') But the most abused prescription drug of the 1970s was the tranquilizer, Valium. Doctors dosed it out like aspirin to patients for almost any medical aliment. We swallowed Valium for headaches, colds, depression, to name a few symptoms, in addition to anxiety for which it was supposed to be prescribed. (Later, an exposé came out that unscrupulous drug salesmen were pressured to generate a billion dollar industry for the pharmaceutical companies by pushing their product onto the medical profession and its providers for off-label indications.)[Ψ] Ten years later specialized drugs like Prozac and other SSRI brands became the optimal medication prescribed for widespread mental depression.

Meanwhile, as time is the best healer, I recovered from my depression. Still young and single, I lived a bon vivant lifestyle, dating and frequenting late night dance clubs and private parties.

At a Hollywood agent's party in Beverly Hills, I met Phyllis Davis, an actress who had starred in a few B movies, notably, Russ Meyers's (unofficial sequel) *Return to the Valley of the Dolls*, which, in twenty years would become a cult film about the 1970s. In the next few months, Phyllis

---

[Ψ] Glazek, Christopher. "The Secretive Family Making Billions From the Opioid Crisis." *Esquire* Nov. 2017.

and I became close friends and I moved into her Beverly Hills, three-bedroom, rose garden house in Coldwater Canyon she rented from Academy Award–winning cinematographer, Ernest Lazlo. Phyllis knew how to promote herself with Hollywood royalty, and dated (slept with) many celebrities. Soon after we met, Phyllis hooked up with Dean Martin by befriending Mort Viner, Dean's manager, who arranged a date for her as soon as Dean broke up dating a blonde actress.

Phyllis told me she had slept with Dean after dinner on their first date together, "You don't play games with Dean Martin." She began seeing Dean exclusively, and before long, Phyllis had moved into Dean's house, leaving me to live alone in the Coldwater Canyon house with her Siberian husky, Clyde, my poodle, and a Himalayan cat.

Phyllis had come to Hollywood when she was eighteen from a little town in West Texas where her family ran a funeral parlor business. She instinctively knew how to find a wealthy, sugar daddy to support her in the luxurious and lavish lifestyle to which she felt entitled. She assured everyone she *really* loved Dean. Who wouldn't love Dean Martin? Of all the film stars, actors, and celebrities I got to know personally, Dean Martin was the nicest and most authentic—Dean was a genuine gentleman. For the record, Dean was not the swaggering, boozehound persona he put on for his Vegas act with his Rat Pack pals, Frank Sinatra, Sammy Davis, Jr., and Peter Lawford. But Dean did abuse pain pills. Phyllis said he took up at least eight a day, which often left him lethargic, but not completely incoherent, due to his high tolerance after years of using them. Phyllis asked me to find Percodan for Dean, a brand of oxycodone—Dean's preferred anodyne. (Mort Viner told me Dean started taking pain pills after he had surgery on his stomach for ulcers; accordingly, from the harrowing twenty years he had partnered with his show-biz cohort, Jerry Lewis, the clown of their act.[9]) But how could I score the controlled substance Rx, Percodan, if Dean Martin couldn't get his own drugs?

---

9 Arthur Marx. *Everybody Loves Somebody Sometimes (especially himself)*: *The Story of Dean Martin and Jerry Lewis*, New York: Hawthorn Books (1974)

While living in Coldwater Canyon, my agent sent me on an audition for an ABC sitcom pilot (situation comedy), and I got the role of Rhonda, a bit dim, blond nurse who worked in a Bronx hospital emergency room. The series aired for eight episodes that fall season, but the network didn't pick it up. I went back pounding the boards (N.Y. metaphor for going on auditions) but I had saved money from the series, and had something to fall back on.

In time, I was cast in more TV roles, including *The Rockford Files,* in which I played a dancer named Belle LaBelle. Filming a special scene with Jim Garner and Tom Selleck was a pleasure. That episode was listed as one of the ten best of the long running series. James Garner and Dean Martin were both *la crème de la crème* of all the actors I met.

The Rockford Files: my role as "Belle Labelle," James Garner and Tom Selleck

On Friday and Saturday nights, I often went to a popular nightclub, or was invited to a private house party in Beverly Hills or in its residential canyons. At his agent's party, I met Richard Beymer, who'd starred in *West Side Story* with Natalie Wood and *The Diary of Anne Frank*. Richard asked for my number. When he called, I invited him to come over to the house in Coldwater Canyon after Phyllis had gone to live with Dean Martin.

When Richard arrived he looked at the winding canyon road and hillside from the front yard, and asked if I knew that the Charles Manson murders took place in Benedict Canyon, the canyon parallel to Coldwater. I was living in Beverly Hills that night in August 1969 when the Manson massacre took place, but I didn't know exactly where the killings happened until Richard told me. He also knew Sharon Tate long before she become a movie star and then brutally murdered, along with four houseguests, during the infamous, summer night that ended the decade of flower power in America.

As a young actor, Richard Beymer was working in a film in Italy when he saw a stunning young teenager on the set that had been hired as an extra. She was a American girl named Sharon Tate who was living in Italy while her father was stationed at a U.S. Army base. Impressed by Sharon's outstanding natural beauty, Richard told her to give him a call if she ever got to Hollywood and he would introduce her to his agent. When Sharon turned eighteen, she persuaded her parents to allow her to go to Los Angeles where she planned to take up Richard's offer and become an actress.

Richard Beymer kept his promise and introduced Sharon to his agent, who immediately signed the young beauty and started sending her on auditions. Before long, film producer, Marty Ransohoff saw the beautiful starlet's potential and signed her to a seven-year contract with Filmways with his intention of making Sharon into a major star. After filming movies in L.A. and London, including *The Fearless Vampire Killers*, directed by (her future husband) Roman and *The Wrecking Crew* with Dean Martin, Sharon was cast as the gorgeous, but fatal, actress in the film of the best-seller novel, *The Valley of the Dolls*.

While filming *Vampires* in London, Roman Polanski and Sharon Tate had fallen in love and got married in Rome. A year later on August 10,

1969, while Roman was in London on business, his eight-month pregnant wife, Sharon, and her unborn son were savagely murdered in a
leased home on Cielo Drive in Benedict Canyon along with four house
guests: a Russian friend of Roman's; hairstylist Jay Sebring; coffee heiress, Abigail Folger; and a young man visiting the property's caretaker.
I remember being in L.A. at the time of the massacre, and was terri-
fied (along with the entire city) after another home invasion-murders
happened the following night in the upscale, Los Felix neighborhood.
Eventually, the savage killers were arrested, along with their cult leader,
Charles Mansion; but in 1969, Sharon Tate's sudden death ended acid-
head, Timothy Leary's mantra, "Turn on, Tune in, and Drop out." The
hippy era of "make love, not war" and 1960s love-ins had reached its
expiration date.

● ● ●

When I was still living in the rented house in Coldwater Canyon after
Phyllis Davis had moved in with Dean Martin, she would often
invite his manager, Mort, and me to join them for dinner at Dean's favorite Italian restaurants, Carmine's or La Famiglia in Beverly Hills.

As his dinner date, Mort told me stories about being a young agent
at the William Morris Agency. He had often driven an ambitious starlet
named Marilyn Monroe to auditions that her agent, Johnny Hyde, had
set up for her. Mort would wait for Marilyn in the outer office when
she was reading a script for the director or casting agent. Once, Mort
heard noises that sounded like sex was happening inside the closed
door. When Marilyn came out, Mort told her that she "didn't have to do
that anymore," now that she had a number of successful credits on her
résumé. Marilyn tossed it off, "Oh, I know, but it's fun!"

Mort told me he also managed the career of Shirley MacLaine and
Dancing in the Rain star, Gene Kelly, along with his super star, Dean Martin.
He negotiated production packages, in which his corral of actors worked
together, like the comedy, *What a Way to Go*, and other studio films.

Once when we were all having dinner at Carmine's, Dean began to doze off, almost falling into his plate of Linguine Alfredo. His glass of vodka on the rocks was still half-full; it was mostly combination of pain pills with a bit of booze that knocked him for a loop. When Dean revitalized, Mort took the keys to his Stutz Bearcat and drove Dean and Phyllis back to Dean's house in Beverly Hills while I drove myself home. As Dean's manager, Mort took good care of his multi-talented client. (When Dean died several years later, Mort was mortally bereft; Dean (his raison d'être) gone, Mort passed away soon after.)

In the meantime Mort and I both noticed Phyllis getting more controlling of Dean, monitoring his whereabouts and listening in on his phone calls. Eventually, Dean began to tire of her ever-tightening reins. He couldn't get away from his live-in girlfriend except on the golf course, and even there, Phyllis had lookouts report back to her if Dean had talked to any women.

It all came to a head when Dean was booked for his annual headline show at the MGM Grand Hotel and Casino in Las Vegas. When Dean got into the limo to catch a plane to Vegas, he told Phyllis to stay in L.A., but she refused to get out the backseat. Irritated, Dean got out of the limo and had Mort drive him to the airport in his car. Unwavering, Phyllis followed Dean to Vegas and got to the MGM Grand Hotel at the same time as Dean—who continued to ignore her.

Accompanied by Mort, Dean hurried through the crowd on the MGM casino floor to the elevators as Phyllis stalked closely behind them. When Dean refused to turn around and talk to her, Phyllis yelled above the clang of the casino slot machines:

"Is this what I get after nine months of sucking your cock?"

Embarrassed by her outburst, Dean pulled his collar up over his ears as he hurried into the elevator door and pressed the button to the penthouse suite. He didn't take Phyllis's constant calls or allow her to come near him for the rest of the week as he performed his hit songs in the headline show in the MGM Grand auditorium.

After this histrionic incident, Dean broke up with Phyllis; but she would not let go. When the lease was up on the Coldwater Canyon house, Phyllis rented another closer to Dean's house in the high-end Trousdale Estates in Beverly Hills with her intentions to get Dean back, but that never happened. He'd had it.

• • •

When I moved out of the house on Coldwater Canyon, I leased a double suite in the once grand–now faded–Garden Court Hotel on Hollywood Boulevard. The older suites had been designed in art deco with a full kitchen, Murphy bed, a latticed, wrought-iron balcony, and original, *fin de siècle* bathroom with a porcelain, pedestal sink and bathtub, and hexagon-tiled walls and floor. Built in 1917, the Garden Court was located across the street from the famous Hollywood Roosevelt hotel and a few doors from Grauman's Chinese Theater, the famous tourist attraction with its forecourt of hand and shoeprints of iconic movie stars with their signatures imprinted in cement. In the early days of Hollywood, the Garden Court Hotel had been a temporary residence to silent-screen stars, e.g., Rudolph Valentino, Clara Bow, and the MGM mogul, Louis B. Mayer. Silver screen director, Max Sennett, lived on the top floor penthouse while he worked on *The Keystone Kops* films.

An episode of *The Rockford Files* was filmed at the Garden Court because it resembled a foregone era in L.A. When the film crew broke for lunch, the star of the series, James Garner, remembered me from the episode, "White on White And Nearly Perfect," that we had filmed for *Rockford* and suggested we have a hot fudge sundae at the historic C. C. Brown's Ice Cream parlor next door on Hollywood Boulevard. In earlier years, C. C. Brown's had been a popular hangout for celebrities like Mary Pickford, Joan Crawford, and Bob Hope. Marlon Brando and his kids became regulars in the 1960s. Brando would take his hot fudge sundae to his limo to avoid the fanfare. While we enjoyed our fudge sundaes, Jim said that he and his wife were currently separated, but he hoped they would get back together soon; and they eventually did. Married to Lois since 1956, James Garner died in their Los Angeles home in 2014.

• • •

Twelve

The Manhattan Project was the code name to develop
the first atomic bomb during World War II.

While living in the Garden Court Apartments on Hollywood
Boulevard, I became friends with Pamela Lambert, a pencil-slim, aging actress who lived down the hall in a single suite with a large cat, named Maurice, after the French matinee idol, Maurice Chevalier. Pamela's role model was actress, Claudette Colbert, whom she idolized. Pam wore her ebony black hair in a pageboy fashioned after the silent screen star, Louise Brooks, with straight bangs cut above her moon-struck, brown eyes and alabaster white complexion.

Pamela told me she had been signed under a seven-year contract with Twentieth Century Fox studios in the 1950s. After earning a living as an actress until the early '60s, she and her two Hungarian husbands had drunk the best liquor and had gone through Pam's generous trust fund years twenty years before I met her. At the time, Pam was subsisting on government disability checks for her severe agoraphobia. Pam couldn't go to the mailbox in the downstairs lobby without first taking a Valium.

Pamela also had a couple of exotic surnames from her two ex-husbands, but I knew her as Pamela Lambert, a stage name she used in the old studio system. Pam had been under contract at Fox at the same time as Marilyn Monroe and had attended many of the studio acing classes with the rising blond movie star. Other actresses under contract at Twentieth Century Fox that time included Joanne Woodward, Susan Hayward, and Jayne Mansfield, who were cast in the lead roles for women while Pam was relegated smaller parts at Fox. When television began producing more programs for an exponentially growing audience, Pam got work in popular, episodic TV shows; she often played roles in Rod Serling's *The Twilight Zone*. Pam was definitively cast for the science fiction series.

Pamela had grown up with a father in show business; he was the radio's "Mr. Dooley, The Answer Man." Her dad had had a successful career in CBS radio in the 1930s. Any on-air question submitted to Mr. Dooley was invariably answered correctly. Pam's mother had told her, "Your father was born knowing everything." As a consequence, Pam's dad had made a lucrative living in radio until one day after one libation too many–and too often–he got into a boisterous altercation with the head of Columbia, CEO William S. Paley, in the cavernous lobby of CBS studios in New York City. (William Paley was the founder of Columbia Broadcasting System, which he had built up from a small radio station into one of the foremost radio and television network operations in America.)

A very drunk Mr. Dooley-Answer Man pushed CEO Bill Paley over a staircase railing in the Manhattan CBS studios. Without notice, Mr. Dooley was summarily fired by CBS, and his name was expunged at Columbia.

After drinking-himself-fired from other less-prestigious radio stations around the country, Mr. Dooley landed a job at a local radio station in Spokane, Washington, in the early 1940s. Pam's father relocated to the eastern Washington state town, taking his wife and young daughter with him. The Hanford Army Base was a two-hour drive from Spokane where her father's cousin, General Leslie Groves, was head of a US Army Corps classified project. General Groves hired Pam's father to work on the secret project and Pam often visited him on the Hanford Army base. She remembered walking around the army base when she was seven years old in her Mary Jane patent leather shoes, Margaret O'Brian hat, and Shirley Temple purse that contained a crisp, new fifty-dollar bill. Not long after WWII ended, Pam's parents divorced. When she turned eighteen, Pamela persuaded her mother to buy her a train ticket to Hollywood where she could pursue her dream of becoming an actress.

· · ·

In the summer of 1987 I read Martin's short story, "Insight at Flame Lake" in *Vanity Fair* and immediately waxed enthusiastic about it to Pamela. Briefly, it involved a young boy and a baby girl living in their parents' lake house in Cape Cod. The boy has a premonition of a nuclear holocaust and its radiation fall-out slowly pervading the atmosphere. After Pam read the short story she asked me where Martin had gotten the name for the character, Sheriff Groves. She had heard the name "Graves" as a surname, but not "Groves." Meanwhile, Martin and I were conversing regularly by telephone, so the next time we talked, I asked him how he came up with Groves for the sheriff in "Flame Lake." He said he had taken it from General Leslie Groves who had been in charge of the Manhattan Project.

When I told Pam where Martin had gotten the name Groves, I asked her why she wanted to know. She revealed for the first time since I met her that Groves was her family name—her maiden name was Pamela Groves—and her father was a scion of "the Groves Family of Kansas City." Not only Pam's birth name but about the prominent Groves family. Mostly, that her father's first cousin was General Leslie S. Groves, head of the Manhattan Project—the secret code for the atomic bomb.

The Manhattan Project was under the administration of the US Army Corps of Engineers, led by General Leslie S. Groves. During 1942–1946, General Groves recruited his paternal cousin, Pamela's father, to work on the top-secret, plutonium project at the Hanford army base in Washington State. America's war efforts during World War II expedited the prompt promotion of Pam's father to Lieutenant Colonel Groves in the US Army so another superior intelligence of the Groves' family genes could be utilized in the classified Manhattan Project.[10]

• • •

In 1982 the Garden Court Hotel and Apartments was listed in the National Register of Historic Places, but this did not prevent the building from being eventually demolished. A corporation developer bought the valuable real estate located next to iconic landmarks on Hollywood Boulevard and constructed the Hollywood Entertainment Museum. An extensive, three-story complex of commercial enterprises, chain stores, and cinemas replaced the once famous Garden Court Hotel. The new complex stands next to Madame Tussaud's Wax Museum and Mann's Chinese Theater, which remains a famous tourist attraction for its celebrated, cement courtyard of movie star hand and shoe prints, and frequent, red carpet, major studio film premieres.

Prior to its being demolished, residents at the Garden Court received a notice from the persnickety old landlord and his wife announcing they were selling the building and had thirty days to vacate the premises.

---

10 After World War II ended, Hanford, WA continued work on creating material for nuclear weapons during the Cold War between the United States and the Soviet Union. With the fall of the USSR and tear down of the iron curtain, Berlin Wall in 1991, Hanford became the largest nuclear contamination site in the United States. Its mission changed from plutonium production to environmental cleanup and restoration. Controversy over the leftover radioactivity in Hanford and the nearby hills of Richmond and its surroundings prompted a massive $112 billion cleanup and with an estimated completion date of 2065. Hanford, WA. *Nuclear Waste Clean Up*: https://en.wikipedia.org/wiki/Hanford_Site

Soon after the tenants left, dozens of homeless and wayward street kids from Hollywood Boulevard discovered the building had been abandoned, and moved inside the dilapidated, vacant rooms to inhabit for free, carouse, drink, use drugs, and co-mingle until they too, were forced to leave. Finally empty of all inhabitants–except for rats and mice– the Garden Court hotel was razed to the ground.

Within the thirty days notice, I had relocated to Beverly Hills, and rented a one-bedroom apartment in a charming, 1920s garden residence on McCarty Drive behind Neiman Marcus department store on Wilshire Boulevard. I heard that actress, Myrna Loy, had lived in the building early in her career before she became famous in *The Thin Man* films with William Powell. More recently, the versatile actor, James Woods had lived there. When I ran into James at Nate's Deli in Beverly Hills, he told me he had moved because the trees outside his windows along the sidewalk had been cut down and street traffic disturbed his formerly quiet apartment. I was living in an upper apartment when I first read Martin's short story and wrote a letter to him.

• • •

When I met the great comedian, Richard Pryor, he was recovering from severe burns after a near-fatal fire accident. Richard described the mishap that almost killed him as "cooking in his room" (he didn't mention it was crack cocaine he was cooking in a crack-pipe). Richard was a gentleman, and although he didn't have a formal education, he was exceptionally intelligent. Also I remember how beautiful Richard's hands were; his long, mocha-hued fingers tapered at the ends like summer willows.

I went out with Richard a couple times and liked him very much. We shared a lot in common—a dark sense of humor, a love of animals, and we both passionately against any form of animal cruelty. His last wife, Jennifer, took up animal causes for Richard, and was active in Los Angeles dog rescue organizations.

One evening Richard picked me up in front of the Beverly Wilshire hotel in his dandelion-yellow Rolls Royce sedan and drove to The San Fernando Valley to see *The Karate Kid.*

Richard wanted to see his actor-friend, Pat Morita, who starred in the film. Standing in line at the cinema for tickets, people began to recognize the comedian star. All of a sudden, a horde of moviegoers swarmed Richard, separating us in the mob. Richard yelled my name above the throng of fans flocking him, reaching up his hand to grab my hand in the crowd. Finally, the fans left us alone and we went into the theater and watched the film in relative peace.

Afterwards, we drove to West Hollywood to dine at the Japanese Gardens restaurant on Sunset Boulevard. Richard tipped the waitresses two hundred dollars, twice the amount of our meal. Attired in formal Japanese kimonos, the grateful Geishas bowed and thanked the generous, Mr. Pryor: *Domo arigato.*

A few days later Richard invited me to visit his home in the San Fernando Valley. When I drove up to the driveway in front of a brick wall surrounding the grounds of his estate in Encino, I buzzed for Richard to open the gates and entered his compound. Richard took me through the house into his backyard to show me the swimming pool he was having rebuilt, and complained how long it was taking to finish. Hundreds of bricks were scattered inside and around the empty pool among piles of dirt beside freshly dug holes. The excavated swimming pool was not near completion—and didn't look like it was designed well. It came across more like a money pit than a swimming pool. The outlay of the scene made me think of a plot pitch for Larry David's TV sitcom, "Curb Your Enthusiasm." Poor, rich Rich.

Richard shared stories about people who had taken advantage of him, using him for connections, borrowing money that had not been repaid, and exploiting him for their own purposes. He said many of his black friends had been the most disappointing because he thought he could trust them. Richard had been married several times—twice to white women; he joked he could get away with more shenanigans with his white wives, using the excuse, "It's a black thing, baby." You have to hand it to Rich.

We spent hours enjoying a light dinner of leftovers in the fridge and laughing. I told Richard the bedtime story of "Little Red Riding Hood," putting a salacious spin on the medieval tale. It seemed to please him more than sex. After hours of fun I tucked Richard into bed and drove home. Richard was a fascinating but complex man.

During our talks together, I lamented, "My life is a cosmic joke." Richard asked me to explain what that meant, so I told him its metaphysical meaning. Later, while passing a newsstand I read the headline in the entertainment section of the L.A. newspaper: "Richard Pryor exclaims, 'My Life is a Cosmic Joke!'" That was Richard—a true gem.

Richard contracted Multiple Sclerosis in his late-forties and was eventually confined to a wheelchair by the 1990s. Richard had remarried Jennifer Lee and she took care of Rich until he died of a heart attack on December 10, 2005. Everyone misses this inimitable man—and so do I.

• • •

Thirteen

FREE RANGE TO NO GLOVE, NO LOVE

*These are the seven deadly sins: venality, paranoia,
insecurity, excess, carnality, contempt, boredom. So
I am lonely, but not alone, like everybody else.*

—*MARTIN AMIS*

By now I was in my early thirties and realized I was dating young men who were, in the words of English author, Barbara Pym, "Unsuitable." They definitely weren't "marriage material."

The crucial question: Was a passionate affair with an exciting lover worth the agonizing aftermath of its breakup? I'd had enough emotional suffering after a superficial relationship with unsuitable, young men had ended. It finally dawned on me that the word *relationship* was a term that basically involved continuous dating, but it did not necessarily imply commitment—at least, not on the part of the men I dated. You hoped your current boy friend was not sleeping with anyone else, but with the ultra-permissive morals at the time and the cornucopia of pretty, young women, "Boys would be boys." It was even likely that one or more of my boyfriends had slept with other men as well as women.

Looking back at 'fast times at Hollywood High' I reflected, "What was I thinking?" The answer is I wasn't. The effect of my cyclic relationships was the agony and the ecstasy of young love. Bad boys were my tragic flaw. Was it possible, at least, unconsciously, that I wasn't looking for a stable relationship? I know there are psychological reasons that explain it.

The fertile environment of stockpiles of young women in Hollywood was a bachelor's paradise and difficult for many to be monogamous. A lot of men took advantage of women in this free-love utopia. The old adage rang true: "Why buy the cow…?" Why, indeed? After the sexual revolution of the 1960s, a woman (in big cities and party towns) was hesitant to ask for sexual exclusivity with their partner—it might scare a man away, heaven forbid. The neologism, "commitment-phobic," was coined because so many women were available on the urban landscape that men didn't want to commit to one when he could have many—especially in Hollywood where new faces arrived every day.

The 1960s until the '80s presented a perfect storm "for fun and for free" sex. Women were willing to make love vis à vis the fierce competition during this permissive era. Hollywood has continuously been flooded with pretty, young women since the beginning of the movie industry in the early 1900s when film studios migrated from New York to California. L.A. men were called "passive conquistadors" because they enjoyed the luxury of seducing women with little effort, especially in these prosperous times. "Sex, drugs, and rock-and-roll" became the slogan for young, urban America in the latter half of the twentieth century. In London too, where a famous young author, Martin Amis, was getting plenty of action.

Then, out of nowhere, a *deus ex machina* brought the age of "unbridled fornication" (to use Marlon Brando's term) to a dramatic downshift. A deadly, unknown disease, at first called "the gay cancer" had become epidemic in the gay community and was killing off male homosexuals in rampant numbers. Soon after, the unexplainable disease began to show up in the heterosexual populations on the urban landscape. Toward the end of the twentieth century, sex with partners outside monogamy had rules.

Within a few years, the carefree days of promiscuous sex were considered reckless and dangerous. Sexual activity in all ranges of demographics was now threatened by the fear of AIDS, the now-diagnosed, incurable STD. From then on, sex between partners required a condom.

"No glove, no love," became the mandatory prerequisite for consensual sex—or the commitment of exclusivity to one partner.

Abstinence was not a solution for most people. In any event, like everyone who wanted to avoid the risk of contracting AIDS and suffering its long, excruciating death, I adopted good, old-fashioned morals and put the brakes on my sequential dating.

Consequently I also decided to change my unproductive choices in my ongoing quest to find a nice guy. It was not long after determining a new criterion for a soul mate that I met a tall, good-looking, young artist named Greg at a skating party given by Ed Begley, Jr., son of former character actor, Ed Begley. Like his father, Ed Junior was a busy, working actor who held an annual roller-skating party in "The Valley" (the San Fernando Valley, due north of L.A.) for his Hollywood actor friends. Malcolm McDowell, Roseanne Barr, Michael Madsen, Michelle Phillips, A and B-listers came to skate at Ed's party. Nicaraguan-beauty, Bianca Jagger (Mick's first wife) was skating alone around the rink; her café au lait complexion was flawless. (More about Bianca later.)

A young artist Greg who worked for Ed Ruscha, L.A.'s most famous modern artist went to the party with Ed's invitation, and we met while watching other skaters in the rink. After talking for a while, Greg asked for my phone number. A week later he invited me to dinner, and we began to see each other exclusively.

• • •

In the summer of 1987 Greg and I had been dating for several months when I happened to read a short story in *Vanity Fair* by a British writer, Martin Amis. The story struck, to quote Shakespeare, "In my heart's core, ay, in my heart of heart," and I felt compelled to write the author in care of his publisher. A month later, when Greg and I returned from a weekend in Mexico, I found a reply from the author in my mailbox. In his brief letter, Martin Amis wrote he would give me an interview and to call him. This unexpected windfall empowered me to be more confident. Greg had been emotionally unavailable during our six-month relationship, and I had accepted his demeanor without asking more. I had gone along with Greg's artistic temperament, and accepted that art was his goal, and thus, priority. But now, he was going to fly to New York with his mentor, Ed Ruscha, to attend Ed's One-man Show at the prestigious Leo Castelli Art Gallery. An elite party at Elaine's, the *au courant,* celebrity restaurant in Manhattan, would follow the art show and he wasn't taking me! Greg said he was Ed's guest, so he couldn't invite anyone. Then I announced I was going fly to London to interview author, Martin Amis, while Greg was in New York; our planes would cross each other mid-way over America as mine flew to London and his returned to L.A. Greg didn't like the idea, and said,

"I can see the writing on this wall."

"I don't know what you're talking about." But, of course, I did.

Greg and me in Mexico

Fourteen

TIME'S ARROW

*Probably human cruelty is fixed and
eternal. Only styles change.*

— *MARTIN AMIS*

Martin sent a letter dated April 9, 1991, from his writing flat to announce he had just finished the novel, *Time's Arrow*, that morning. He said it had been driving him crazy for two years, and the last eight months had been driving him even more crazy—in the last four or five weeks he had gone absolutely bonkers to finish the story of a Nazi doctor told in reverse time. The subject had been exasperating to write—even more, writing it in a backward-in-time sequence. Martin said he'd been warned that anyone writing about the Holocaust could not sleep well for at least a year or two and now he believed it. To get away and return to a semblance of normal, he planned a short trip to Spain and Italy. Martin enjoyed our telephone conversation and thought I sounded good—he closed with, Love Martin X.

• • •

Julia Clinch

When his novel, *Time's Arrow* [12] was ready for the publisher's galley, Martin sent me a copy of the proof from London.

He included a letter inside the proof saying the novel was conclusive evidence of his painful preoccupation. Now finished, he was flying to Cape Cod in New England with his family to spend the last of the summer at his in-laws' beach home. His oldest son had had a successful eye operation, which was a huge relief. Martin promised to write when he returned from his summer on the East Coast and hoped to be coming to L.A. in the autumn.

The narrative of *Time's Arrow* was about a Nazi doctor who had worked in a German concentration camp during World War II—told backwards in time. Martin spun the Nazi doctor's life around, beginning with the old man on his deathbed in New York where he had immigrated shortly after the war. His life is revealed in reversed-time sequences as years flow backward from his life in America to Nazi Germany when he was a young doctor in the death camps. As time's arrow points in the opposite direction, instead of watching trains bringing tens of thousands of Jews to concentration camps, the doctor watches these same trains taking Jews away—back to the cities, towns, and farms where they had lived in prewar Europe. Essentially, reversing time's arrow expunges the Holocaust.

Martin has labeled himself a "philo-semite," or, as he says, he loves Jews. Is Martin's pro-Jewish sentiment his personal apology for Hitler's Final Solution to annihilate the Jews in Europe? Although Martin cannot fathom the evil methodology of the Holocaust, he strives to understand it. Martin reminds us what Primo Levi pointed out: "If we were to understand the Holocaust, it would diminish our humanity." Exploring man's predisposition to do evil, he wants to understand why some human beings descend to its abject enormities. For that matter, what impels Martin Amis to ponder man's depravity?

Like the nineteenth-century Russian author, Fyodor Dostoyevsky, Martin is passionate about the question of evil as a subject; both focus on the nadir of human nature: Why does a man choose evil over goodness?

---

12 Martin Amis, *Time's Arrow*. London: Jonathan Cape, Ltd., 1991.

And, when he does, how much evil can he bestow on his fellow man? Martin believes the Jewish Holocaust came as close to fundamental evil on a systematic scale as ever-recorded in history. In *Time's Arrow*, Amis rectifies the twentieth-century tragedy, by turning time backwards to undo the ultimate crime against Jews.

In his book, *How Could This Happen: Explaining the Holocaust*, Dan McMillan explores man's inhumanity to man; why the Nazis rose to power in Germany after World War I, and how Hitler became a god to the German people who allowed this demagogue to start a second world war that would decimate the Jewish population and destroy Germany. Under Hitler's orders, Nazis utilized the German ethos for precision and organization to wipe out a generation of European Jews and non-Aryans who were considered undesirable (*untermensch*). More than 90 percent of Europe's Jews were killed in the last few years of World War II.

Upon arriving at concentration camp train stations, Jewish men, women, and children were divided into groups. In Treblinka, Poland's death camp, the first group was immediately ordered to remove their jewelry and shoes, and marched away in single file to a small building with the Star of David above the entrance, so as not to arouse anxiety. Inside an antechamber, this group was told to remove their clothing and hang it on hooks on the wall; and then ordered into a large shower room, which, after they entered, was locked shut. Poison gas immediately began to emerge from faux showerheads affixed on the ceiling, and the killing began.

The camp guards could peer into the shower room through a small, rectangular window as they waited for the cries and screams to eventually silence. The guards quickly removed the still-warm corpses onto open carts on a small railway track to be carried to nearby, pre-dug graves. The entire process took less than an hour. The second group of Jews was assigned to hard labor in the camp, sleeping in cold, barren barracks. Many of the slave laborers were worked to death or died from unsanitary conditions in the camp from typhus or infectious diseases.

Continuing with the theme of the Holocaust, Martin's later novel, *Zone of Interest* (2014) takes place in the Auschwitz concentration camp. Although it got good reviews, *Zone of Interest,* has been mildly received publicly. Martin writes in *Zone of Interest,* *"Hitler not only wants to wipe out Jews but is also intent on destroying Germany. He has a final solution for every-one, all of whom must look in a mirror and see his or her soul."* Coincidentally, it was the intention of Hitler (whom Amis never names in *Zone of Interest*) for the Fatherland to fall at the end of the war because he wanted to punish Germans for being weak and losing the war he began. This is logical in the Hitler's delusional, solipsistic thinking.

Martin's penchant to write about (in his words) "the banality of evil," is evident, whether it is the Holocaust or Joseph Stalin in *Koba the Dread: Laughter and the Twenty Million*—about the Ukrainian farmers and their families that Stalin starved to death when he expropriated their grains to fill his Soviet silos. Goodness vs. evil is a predominant theme in Amis's works as his polarized protagonists and dopplegängers go mano a mano with their antagonists.

His authorial ideal, Nabokov, and Martin play good against evil in protagonist vs. foil, each imbued with extreme polarities. Martin said he "piles all the good into one, and all the bad into the other," [Л] creating characters with antithetic qualities; as it were, in *London Fields,* two of Nicola's lovers: the low-life thug, Keith Talent, is opposite of the posh gentleman, Guy Clinch. Martin does the same with two babies in the novel, making Marmaduke the bad seed, and Kathy the perfect child. He draws on opposing economic status—the upper vs. lower classes of society. Martin explained, "The middle class has been fairly well covered enough already."

• • •

Л Concerning Martin's attraction to opposites, he stated, "DeLillo reached a conclusion that I share. I think it's in *London Fields,* that, put it this way, love has two opposites. One is hatred and one is death. And death and love are opposite in our internal cosmologies." – Martin Amis Talks Terrorism, Pornography, Idyllic Brooklyn, and American: by David Wallace-Wells in *New York* Magazine, July 2012.

Fifteen

TIME'S ARROW STOPS IN L.A.

*People look at fame and feel deprived if they haven't
got it, feeling that this is a basic, almost a human
right, a civil right. And also feel the same way
about wealth, I suppose - why haven't I got it?*

– MARTIN AMIS

Martin was scheduled to stop in Los Angeles on March 29, 1991, on his American book tour for his new novel, *Time's Arrow*. He called the week before to invite me to have dinner with him. Delighted I would see him soon, I wished him well. Martin planned to arrive at LAX the night before the reading and check into the Beverly Wilshire Hotel where his publisher had booked him.

A few months prior, Martin had sent me the proof of *Time's Arrow*. After reading it, I sent him a letter:

Dear Martin,

Received the proof of *Time's Arrow* and I'm happy to see your talent has not mitigated nor your genius paled. I am just recovering from the explosive impact of this novel. It reminds me of Joyce's *Ulysses* in terms of experimental stream of consciousness, except that time flows backward.

Seeing reports on television of Hurricane John at Cape Cod, and a second Russian Revolution going on in the Soviet Union during your vacation, I wonder now if you are of the same opinion that holidays that go haywire are more interesting than those where all goes as planned.

I hope your plane lands safely and no more mid-flight surprises like the one you had. Please keep me posted on your L.A. visit.

Well, dear friend, thanks again for your new novel.

Love, Julie

P.S. Enclosed please find the *L.A. Times* review of *Barbara Pym's Diaries* that label Kingsley Amis's novels as misogynist. *

*Note: Martin later told me what his father said when he showed the book review to him; Sir Kingsley retorted, "Who said *that?* – some *feminist?*"

When Martin came to L.A. on his book tour for *Time's Arrow*, I was living in a residential area on the West end of Hollywood Boulevard, close to the major tourist spots—the Walk of Fame, star-studded sidewalks engraved with celebrity names on the famous boulevard. Famous actors who had graced the screen over the last hundred years had their own bronze stars on Hollywood Boulevard. Grauman's Chinese Theater was a stone's throw away where movie stars signed their names and embedded their hand and shoe prints in cement in the front walkway. My apartment was ten minutes to the center of glamorous Tinseltown where major film premiers and annual award ceremonies were held: the Emmys, Grammies, and Academy Awards. The renowned boulevard also attracted undesirable elements: the motley rabble of drug dealers, prostitutes, teenage runaways, and drifters that trickle in from all over America and the world.

Stories that romanticize the downside of Hollywood Boulevard, like the film, *Pretty Woman*, starring Julia Roberts, happen in movies, not in real life. The film glorified the life of a young prostitute, played by Julia who meets and marries a handsome, rich 'john' (Richard Gere). Hollywood hookers have the same chance of winning the lottery as marrying the man Gere portrayed. Besides, these errant, young women will not stay pretty or young for long.

I always considered the fairytale film a travesty for enticing young women to come to Hollywood with its misleading, delusional Cinderella plot. A streetwalker who ends up marrying a handsome, rich man is not likely, even in a fairytale. Most often, a hooker on Hollywood Boulevard will become a drug addict, beaten up by a john or her pimp, or dead.

Hollywood film moguls and marketers decided long ago what moviegoers would spend their money on. Movie studios intend to give the audience what they want: a happy ending. Studios and independent productions continue to crank out films that propagate whimsical scenarios about love, knowing a romantic comedy like *Pretty Woman,* starring popular actors like Julia Roberts and Richard Gere is a sure investment for a box office draw with good profits.

Young men and women arrive daily in Hollywood from all over the world, seeking their vision of the American Dream. They've been coming ever since the invention of the 'moving pictures' camera in the early 1900s to work on the silver screen—that was replaced by "talkies;" added sound first appeared in Al Jolson's *The Jazz Singer* in 1927. Every one of these novices believed he or she had what it took to become a movie star.

Some of the young men who flocked to Hollywood with big dreams made a name for themselves: Rudolph Valentino from Italy; Humphrey Bogart from New York; Australian-born swashbuckler, Errol Flynn; and Iowa native, John Wayne all started their careers with small roles in B movies. Young men still come to Hollywood with their determination to become the next Brad Pitt or Ryan Gosling. One advantage the young men have over the women is they are more realistic about the fame game. Males instinctively know the Faustian sacrifice needed to succeed in Hollywood. The few major exceptions were actresses like Joan

Crawford, Barbara Stanwyck, and Bette Davis who arrived in Hollywood in their early teens and quickly learned how to think like a man.

It took a while working in Hollywood before I acclimated to its peculiar form of reality. I continued acting classes after the ones I'd taken at the UCLA Theater Arts department where I had won the best actress award. In addition to substitute teaching, I made a living in the movie industry, which, according to the Screen Actors Guild, is beating the odds. I took the chance to go for it; I didn't want to be the woman who, at the age of fifty, reflected, "If only..."

Looking back, I wonder if I should have driven to LAX and met Martin the night he walked off the plane. (This was before 9/11 when anyone could go to a flight gate at the airport without a boarding pass.) I distinctly remember deciding not to go to LAX or meet him in the lobby of the Beverly Wilshire where he was booked that night. However, I did call the hotel every half-hour to inquire if Martin Amis had checked in yet. Finally, after 10:00 p.m., Martin picked up the phone in his hotel room. Martin said he had taken a Valium on the plane and was calling it a night after the long flight from the East Coast.

We agreed to have dinner the following night after his reading at a bookstore in West L.A. Since I wasn't going to the reading, Martin told me to meet him in the cocktail lounge off the lobby of the Beverly Wilshire Hotel. I asked him to call and wake me at 10:00 a.m. the next day, but he didn't. Instead, he called around 11:30 a.m. When I asked why he didn't call earlier, he said he had been in a meeting and had an interview with an NPR radio show host in Santa Monica. Later, Martin gave me the tape recording of the show he had with the intellectual interviewer. He said the host kept bringing up esoteric authors like the French writer, Céline, during the interview, trying to tie them into Martin's works. We both laughed. Martin said he liked my questions about his novels much more, citing my question "Did Trish Stewart give Keith Talent a blowjob in the washroom of the Black Cross pub?" in *London Fields*.

I was enamored with Martin's mind, but even if I were attracted to him, not enough time had passed for the next level. When you live and work in Hollywood, you run into a hundreds of male hunks on a regular basis; and although there are a lot of star-f*ckers in this town, I wasn't one. Case in point, twenty years earlier I met Warren Beatty when I was a student at UCLA, and did not go to bed with him…at least, not straightaway.

• • •

I n my junior year at UCLA I was working part-time as a cashier at the Hamburger Hamlet, a trendy restaurant within walking distance of the off-campus apartment I shared with three female roommates. One night, Warren Beatty came in with his longtime girlfriend, Julie Christie, the British actress who had recently won the Oscar for best actress in *Darling*. While Julie was escorted to their table, Warren went up the stairs to the men's room on the mezzanine floor. Seizing the opportunity, I immediately left my post at the cash register, telling a coworker I had to use the restroom, and scampered up the carpeted stairs like a puppy to follow him. I had recently seen Beatty's box-office hit *Bonnie and Clyde*, and I was determined to meet the exciting, young actor.

Ever since high school, I had had a crush on Warren Beatty after I saw him star in the film, *Splendor in the Grass*, with Natalie Wood. This movie made a tremendous impact on my ingenuous mind when I was the same age as the film's teenager lovers, experiencing first love—followed by its intense sorrow. William Inge's screenplay takes its title from William Wordsworth's poem, "Intimations of Immorality," which sentimentalized the idealism of youth:

> "Let us not forget the hour of splendor in
> the grass, and glory in the flower;
> we will grieve not, but find strength in what remains behind."

Young lovers, dashed by the experience of love lost—intensified the loss of idealistic innocence—find reality hard to endure; and some cannot.

Rumor was that Warren had broken Natalie's heart in real life after she had left her first husband, Robert Wagner, to be with him. (Several years later, Natalie remarried Wagner.) Meanwhile, women all over the world had seen the bittersweet film, *Splendor in the Grass,* and were smitten with the young actor—as love-struck women had been fifty years before, who had watched Rudolph Valentino seduce helpless damsels in his desert tent in *The Sheik.*

Waiting outside the men's room for Warren to come out, I stood transfixed when he did. Warren immediately took control of the young woman standing there, asking a barrage of questions, one after the other: "What's your name? Where are you from? How old are you?" A twenty-year-old college girl, nervously face to face of a major movie star, I eagerly answered him.

The cigarettes in the package I held in my hand dropped out onto the floral, crimson carpet, and Warren, a Southern gentleman raised in Virginia, picked them up, and handed each cigarette back to me without missing a beat of the interrogation. The plush, piled carpet beneath us transformed onto a surreal magic carpet ride on which I floated to a virtual cloud nine. Satisfied with my answers and appearance, Warren told me to call him at his penthouse suite at the Beverly Wilshire Hotel.

Fortunately, I was well dressed the night I met Warren. I remember wearing a new cerulean blue knit jacket and skirt my mother had bought me for my twentieth birthday. It took many hits and misses to find what sartorially suited me, but that night, I scored in an outfit that enhanced the glow of young pheromones.

Barely out of my teens, blossoming with feminine hormones, I abashedly confess that if I liked a boy, it wasn't long before we became intimate. The sexual revolution had begun its full swing. However, it took quite a while before I got to know Warren Beatty in the Biblical sense.

After meeting Warren I called him a few days later as requested at the Beverly Wilshire Hotel, and he invited me to come up to his penthouse suite; we agreed on the following afternoon. After going through the hotel lobby, I went into the old elevator still operated by hand by a pretty woman to the penthouse floor, and walked up a divided, white stairwell to the penthouse and knocked on the door. Opening it, Warren greeted me and asked if I wanted anything to drink. I asked for a gin gimlet, which was promptly brought up by a waiter. Nothing transpired physically on my first visit, but we talked for a few hours. I remember Warren staring intensely at me, waiting for me to make a move, but I didn't.

My visits became more frequent over the next several months. On one occasion, when I was starting up the final stairwell to his penthouse, a dark, slim beauty was just leaving. Warren introduced me to the young woman named Bianca. She was visibly piqued that I was about to go in his suite she had just been in. I was naïve about the situation I'd walked into as I held out my hand, saying it was nice to meet her. It didn't enter my mind they'd just had an afternoon assignation because I hadn't (yet), and I was clueless about other people's sexual proclivities.

Later on, Warren referred to the exotic vixen I'd seen at his door. "You know that girl you met, Bianca? She married Mick Jagger." She became his first wife, the well-known Bianca Jagger.

Warren was into who was doing whom in the world of celebrity. It must have been a notch on his bedpost to have had the Nicaraguan beauty before Mick.

When I visited Warren at the Beverly Wilshire, I'd sit demurely on a chair across from him while he sat on the sofa. Meanwhile, Julie Christie was still his one-but-not-only paramour. Once I saw a wooden-beaded purse she had left in his bedroom.

There were only two rooms in his penthouse plus a small kitchenette, a door to the hallway stairs and another door to the outside roof of the large hotel. The outdoors area served as Warren's personal terrace that stretched across the top of the hotel and gave a bird's view to the scenic, panorama of Beverly Hills and the Hollywood Hills. Warren said on a clear day he could see Santa Monica, and even make out the ocean. On sunny afternoons, he would sit al fresco on his terrace in the lone chaise lounge to "get some color" (as told me).

Whenever it came time to leave Warren's penthouse, I was reluctant to go back into the mundane world of reality. Compared to hanging out with a movie star, life seemed dull and prosaic. It was depressing to have to return to the pedestrian and predictable everyday, classes, homework, exams, and prerequisites of college —after being with the larger than life luminary.

Once when I was leaving his penthouse, I told Warren, "I really don't want to go out there. Being with you is like having a feeling of immortality. You're famous, which means you'll live on forever, eons past the little lives of normal people who only have a short time to live under the sun. I don't want to go back to the land of mortality."

Walking me to the door, Warren said, "That's very intelligent of you to recognize that. You're very smart." Perhaps I was—in a philosophical sense, but not much else—not in life or experience.

• • •

One afternoon we were sitting and talking in his penthouse. Finally, Warren confronted me with the elephant in the room,
"So, you still aren't into fucking."
Not expecting the candid statement, I stood my ground and replied, "I am…just not at the moment."
It was obvious that sex was the main reason Warren was interested in me, and I was taking my time…to his chagrin.

Frankly, I'm surprised he allowed my abstinence (with him) to go on for so long. We talked a lot and played mental games that seemed to entertain him. Warren wasn't aggressive, but his conversation was mostly sexual in general. Handsome men who also happen to be rich and famous will wait for women to make the first move. And we eventually do. But I wasn't taking the bait. Warren had invited me into the elite world of personal exclusivity with an A-list celebrity. Unless you were also rich and famous, the prerequisite usually required sex as the initiation fee and I had not paid my dues; it was several months overdue. So I did.

In the next ten years I saw Warren on and off. At times, he drove his black, Lincoln town car to my apartment or to a friend's house where I was staying. A few times I ran into Warren at Hefner's Playboy Mansion. Once I found him cavorting with three young women in one of the Mansion's exterior buildings called the Game House. A tall, blonde with a French accent in Jordache jeans invited me to join them in a ménage in a room near the pinball machines. She opened the door and climbed onto a king-size bed where two girls were lying on each side of Warren. I stood staring in the doorway until Warren told them, "She's not into this scene." That said, I left Warren's ad hoc harem to his own devices, and closed the door.

The *mondo famoso* is an elite world, as it were, a jet-set microcosm of the beau monde that would bring Martin Amis, Warren Beatty, and me together several years later; coincidentally, on another hotel terrace not far from the Beverly Wilshire Hotel. A festive party for Los Angeles illuminati to celebrate the honored guests after an "Evening with Christopher Hitchens and Martin Amis" at UCLA, was held at the W Hotel, a short drive away, over a sweeping hill on the Wilshire Corridor in Westwood Village.

Ironically, this evening I was meeting Martin in the Beverly Wilshire, in which two decades earlier my assignations with Warren had taken place in his penthouse. What would happen tonight with Martin after drinks, conversation and dinner, only the gods knew.

Sixteen

The Last Supper

Martin told me to meet him in the cocktail lounge of the Beverly Wilshire Hotel at 7:30 p.m. He would join me after his reading of *Time's Arrow* in West L.A. Getting ready in my apartment on Hollywood Boulevard, I slipped into a form-fitting, little black dress and arm-length, black cocktail gloves. Charles Jourdan, crystal-studded stilettos and a black Valentino jacket completed the dressed-to-impress look I was going for. I sprayed the entire ensemble with Joop Eau de cologne, my half-brother, Charles, had bought for my birthday at Saks Fifth Avenue in Beverly Hills. I had chosen the French-German fragrance instead of my favorite, Givenchy's Ysatis perfume because Joop had a floral scent with a tinge of the erotic. Before leaving, I applied Guerlain's *Plus Que Jamais Rose* lipstick. I was infatuated with the British author and hoped he liked my soignée.

Driving into Beverly Hills, I parked on a side street rather than using the hotel's valet service. My Japanese car would not fit with the German, Italian, and British luxury models. I was careful not to trip as I stepped over the redbrick, Beverly Wilshire driveway to the hotel entrance. A tall, black doorman in a mustard BW stamped uniform with green piping and yellow tassels on the epaulettes opened the heavy, glass door for me and

I thanked him. I had arrived early and ordered a bottle of Perrier while I waited for Martin at a cocktail table in the newly renovated hotel lounge. Sitting next to a Doric column, I reminisced about my old haunts in the landmark hotel in which I'd spent many nights until closing as a single, young L.A. woman in the glamorous, international setting.

Nostalgia flooded in about friends and lovers I'd met for drinks and dinner in the gone El Padrino room, the theme of which had been the American Southwest, complete with saddles and paintings of the old West. The El Padrino lounge and dining room—where the elite meet to eat— was the designated place for celebrities, movie stars, wealthy hotel guests; and, consequently, by 1979, the newly migrated, dripping-with-money Iranians. These rich Persians had fled Tehran, as rumors turned into reality that the Ayatollah Khomeini and his Islamic revolutionaries would overthrow the last Shah of Iran, Mohammad Reza Shah Pahlavi. The Shah, his family and loyal followers made it out before the once modern Iran was besieged by the fundamentalist Ayatollah's regime to reign over the Islamic Republic of Iran.

A young scion of a wealthy, Iranian dynasty, Majid P., immigrated to Beverly Hills with his father and family. Majid was tall, aristocratically slim, with dark-wavy hair and soft brown eyes, which contrasted with his Aryan fair complexion, and spoke softly in a cadence. Majid and his father chose the Beverly Wilshire El Padrino room as their designated place to meet and entertain after arriving in Beverly Hills.

Soon after I was introduced to Majid in the El Padrino room as he held court at a long table flanked by several young women drinking champagne, and eating hors-d'oeuvres; one cheeky woman was trying to pique his quiet composure. In an aside, Majid invited me to have dinner with him the following night in the dark lounge. I brought along a girlfriend in case Majid would dash off as he had with another woman, leaving her alone with an open tab to order whatever she wanted, including another bottle Dom Perignon. Although quiet, Majid was a charming dinner companion to both my friend and me throughout the evening.

We knew from the international press that Majid and other affluent Iranians had had to leave vast properties and personal treasures in Iran when they quickly immigrated to America before the Shah was deposed. Those who remained in Tehran risked being executed as traitors and loyalists to Shah Pahlavi and his regime. Nevertheless, the upper class ex-patriots did not leave Iran before first transferring multiple millions of liquid assets into Swiss bank accounts.

Majid had a penchant for expensive luxury cars that he collected as a hobby. Among many in his large garage was a customized, red Lamborghini Countach that he had ordered from the Italian factory. While waiting for political asylum in the United States, he had the car flown from Switzerland and imported to Beverly Hills where he and his family eventually immigrated. Majid's car collection included two Lamborghinis, three Ferraris, a black Maserati, two Porsches, and a silver Bentley—all customized to spec—plus a couple of mint Mercedes for quick stops around town. Majid and his father invested more than twenty million 1979 dollars in Beverly Hills commercial real estate and high-end apartment buildings the same year they came to California. A luxurious building on the Wilshire Corridor and a high-rise apartment building on Wilshire Boulevard in Brentwood were turned into multimillion-dollar condos by the end of the eighties. The Iranian family developed several real estate properties and purchased a multimillion-dollar condominium building that remained a steel shell for years. By the end of the decade, Majid and his father's company had invested $500 million in 1980s currency in Beverly Hills and West L.A. commercial real estate.

A dire rumor about Majid was going around some years later according to an acquaintance of his, Doug Dickson, who was Alain Clenet's first financial backer:

"When he was in the Clenet showroom a few weeks ago, Dickson was told that Majid and his father went back to Iran for some reason and were arrested and subsequently beheaded."

A follower on the Ferrari Internet chat room had also heard this rumor and posted, "I will tell you a story about your car's Beverly Hills owner—sometime after the Iranian Revolution, he accompanied Trefor Thomas on a trip back to Iran. Trefor returned, but unfortunately, your car's owner was detained there & [sic] suffered an untimely demise at the hands of the new regime since he was viewed as being a Shah sympathizer. Sad story."

Later, I read that this was not true. Reportedly, in 2017, Majid was very much alive in his sixties, living with his Iranian family in Beverly Hill, as a very rich man.

Martin arrived at the lobby lounge and the hostess brought him to the table. He greeted me affectionately with a kiss on both cheeks before sitting down and ordered a glass of red wine. We exchanged pleasantries and he said his reading went well in West L.A.

I asked him how his father was doing these days. Martian replied he was the same witty curmudgeon, doing as well as could be expected at his age, in his early seventies.

I then asked if his dad would like me.

"I think he's gotten rather past that by now," Martin replied. "You know, he's living in my mother's house with her present husband."

"I didn't mean it in *that* way. Why do men have to put a sexual connotation on everything?" I asked, teasing him.

He smiled at my rejoinder. I doubt Sir Kingsley would have given me a second thought. Finishing his wine, Martin suggested we have dinner in the hotel dining room. When the maître d' took us to our table, Martin ordered a steak—medium rare, as usual—and another glass of cabernet sauvignon. I had the lemon-broiled whitefish and another sparkling water.

After dinner Martin signed the bill on his room number, and we walked outside the hotel across the red brick driveway to the addition, high-rise suites. Once inside the elevator, Martin pushed the seventh-floor button. I remember looking straight into Martin's languorous, gray-blue eyes as we ascended in the small enclosure. With my own height elevated in four-inch heels, my eyes were even with his. Martin is short, but not *that* short, as a former girlfriend wrote; to wit, he is *not* small, a word she also used.

Walking down the gecko-green carpet in the hall, we were both in apprehensive silence until Martin opened the door to his room. Taking off his jacket, Martin immediately poured himself a drink from an open bottle of liquor on a desk. He asked me if I wanted a glass.

"No, thank you." I was still on the wagon.

I could tell Martin was tired. Holding his glass, he circled around the king-size bed. Then suddenly, out of nowhere, he confronted me about our first meeting in London.

"Do you know that you winced when you first saw me at the door?"

Surprised at this sudden outburst, I fell back on the bed where I sat, promptly denying I had any such reaction. (However, I remember averting my eyes when he opened the door.) Martin insisted I had been unprepared for his appearance that bore no resemblance to his photos.

"Nevertheless, I knew I had you in my hand within five minutes," he added, satisfied his spell over women was still intact.

I agreed that he had definitely charmed me; I was, indeed, one of his many virtual conquests.

Excusing myself to go into the bathroom, I closed the door, and observed a display of Martin's toiletries on the marble sink counter. I noticed a tin of tooth powder, rarely seen in America since the 1950s. This archaic dental cleanser reminded me when Martin smiled, his side teeth looked dark and decomposed. Later on, I read how his gums had pained him all his life; and since, his fiancée, Isabel, had taken him to a New York dentist who replaced his "English teeth" (crooked, church-cemetery-tomb-spaced) with prosthetic implants and caps.

When I came back into the room I saw Martin's trousers and shirt strewn over a chair and he lay under the bed covers ready to call it a day.

Turning out the lamplight, I left Martin in bed, soon to be cradled in the arms of Morpheus. On the way out I saw a copy of *Time's Arrow* on a side table. I opened it to see Martin's handwritten annotations and penciled-in notes in the margins and pages. This must have been his copy for the book tour. He would use it for his reading the following night in San Francisco.

• • •

O n 22 December 1991, a London postcard with photos of HRH Majesty Queen Elizabeth II and "Different views of the Queen's Guards" was sent inside a British stamped envelope to my apartment on Hollywood Boulevard where I was living. Martin wrote he was off on holiday to freezing Cardiff to recover from his American tour. He wished me the happiest New Year, and again signed, love, Martin.

• • •

Seventeen

THE RODNEY KING RIOTS: APRIL 1992

The Rodney King riots began in Los Angeles on April 29, 1992, the day after I had moved into an apartment in West Hollywood.

I sent Martin a clipping from *The Los Angeles Times* of a map showing the four areas affected by the Rodney King riots: "The Path of Destruction: Central Los Angeles, Hollywood."

The three days of disorder killed 55 people, injured almost 2,000, led to 7,000 arrests, and caused nearly $1 billion in property damage, including the burnings of nearly four buildings. California Governor Pete Wilson deployed the National Guard at the request of Mayor Tom Bradley, and a curfew was declared. By the morning, hundreds of fires were burning across the city, more than dozens of people had been killed and hundreds were injured. — L.A. Times

The Los Angeles Times article reported the Path of Destruction of the areas of rioting, heavy looting, arson, and fires. One of the places hit by looters was the upscale, high-rise, the Beverly Center: "Southern California's premier fashion destination, with 160 distinctive, specialty boutiques reflecting the diverse styles and tastes of Los Angeles." Coincidentally, the Sofitel Hotel where Martin and I had dinner is across the street on Beverly Boulevard. On the day the riots started I had just moved into an apartment—next to La Cienega Blvd. and the Beverly Center. From the front window I watched hundreds of L.A.'s citizens of all ages, races, and status running amok.

• • •

I wrote Martin: "The riots resulted after the trial of four LAPD policemen found the accused "not guilty." The smell of charred smoke engulfed the atmosphere of the city of Los Angeles for three entire days."

May 7, 1992

Dear Martin,

On the second day after the riots began I watched a dozen, buff-built, young black men in designer sportswear jump out of their open jeeps and cars in the parking lot in front of my apartment building and head toward the Beverly Center. The eager 'gangstas' wore high-top Nikes and hightailed toward the celebrated, high-end fashion mall as fast they could.

Predictably, they were out to loot property, clothing, furnishings; whatever they could carry out from the high-rise complex of designer shops and boutiques. These young African Americans weren't your typical inner city, 'gang-bangers.' It was obvious these young men had money to buy new jeeps, name brand sportswear, hoodies, and high-tops.

The rioters and looters were closing in on city blocks near Beverly Hills by now after the widespread riots and arson had begun. Looting has become a citywide sport without much consequence, if any. The LAPD and fire department were too busy arresting armed rioters and arsonists to keep up with minor crimes and rampant looters in stores. Now that rioters had reached the Beverly Center and my apartment, I could see the young marauders running toward "Southern California's premier fashion destination."

The Beverly Center is L.A.'s citadel of consumerism, second to none. It is an eight-tiered, self-contained fortress of stuff people buy to feel euphoric and self-empowering. An icon of capitalism, entertainment, manmade thrills, the Beverly Center provided constant stimulation with multiple shopping levels inside one huge city block of concrete and glass. Don't get me wrong: it's all class and glass.

Whenever I want to kill a good two hours, I buy a double cappuccino and wander through the aisles of its massive construct, just looking, roaming the exclusive store fronts to the designer boutiques, getting high from the constantly moving visual and audio stimuli. The Beverly Center shoppers and consumers are fascinating to watch as well. It's metaphorically like socially approved porn because when you finally leave this orgiastic utopia and are outside on the street, you feel spent, drained, wiped out. This is no marketing circus; it's a "stately pleasure dome."

The day the riot got into full swing, I had gone to stock up on groceries, not knowing when I'd be able to leave my apartment again. Stores and businesses in the city had already closed down. Heavy chains were wrapped around the push levers on the market's glass double doors. The store manager exhorted the customers outside to return to our homes. I began walking swiftly back to my apartment—off La Cienega Boulevard, the main street that bifurcates Hollywood from Beverly Hills. It seemed as if L.A. had turned into Gotham City. Pedestrians were running around in pandemonium as drivers tried not to hit them as they jaywalked across the boulevard and ran through traffic light signals.

Enraged black men jumped out of their cars, some assaulting shopkeepers who were standing outside trying to protect their stores, yelling hate speech at merchants and anyone who got in their way. I hightailed it home on foot. Turning on TV news, I watched in horror at continuous fires furtively set by angry, black arsonists—strewn with gasoline without fear of restraint or arrest.

Further down Wilshire Boulevard in Little Korea, Korean merchants and store owners were guarding their businesses, some standing on rooftops brandishing loaded Glocks and Smith & Wesson semi-automatics, ready to fire at any violent attack. Continuous film footage from helicopters showed commercial buildings blazing like bonfires on every other block in a city under siege. I had relocated to this apartment the day before the verdict had been announced "Not Guilty" for four policemen who were filmed assaulting Rodney King. The riots started within a few hours after the verdict was read on the news. A violent assault was televised from a helicopter of a white man being attacked by several black men as he drove his truck through an inner city area. Black thugs had pulled the driver out of his truck and mercilessly beat him up. The news showed the scene live from a local news helicopter camera as one attacker picked up a huge cinder block and chucked it on the white man's head as he lay unconscious in the city street.

I haven't slept much since the violence started, it's messed up my sleep cycle. You can call me anytime, morning or night—if the machine answers, talk into it and I'll pick up.

Update a day later: judging from today's promenade outside, life has suddenly settled back to a strange calmness (after the storm). In fact, there's an atmosphere of visceral relief, considering the pervasive smell of charred smoke still in the air and scorched, blackened buildings on the streets from the extensive arson in the past three days.

When I took a walk today, I passed by the Sofitel Hotel and looked up at its tiered stories, wondering if the room you slept in faced the boulevard. It's only a five-minute walk from where I live now.

Love, Julie

• • •

Sent to Times May 4-92
(2 DAYS AFTER THE RIOT)

CONFIDENTIAL:
(213) 852-7177
8456 Blackburn Av.#7
Los Angeles, Ca 90048

May 4, 1992

Editor, L.A. Times
Times Mirror Square
Los Angeles, Ca 90053

Dear Editor,

    As a former school teacher in L.A. Inner City schools and before that, a social worker near Watts, I watched in fear from my apartment hordes of youths, mostly in designer visors and Gap T-shirts and name-brand gym shoes jump out of four-wheel drives newer than my old car looking for trouble and headed for the Beverly Center and other business, markets, and commercial shops on La Cienega. This is it, I thought, as I loaded up, I'm a sitting duck.

    Minutes later I saw these same youths run back to their vehicles and dash away. I looked at La Cienega and saw L.A.P.D. officers arresting suspects and containing the near-by anarchy. My neighbors and I began to be relieved.

    "60 Minutes" tried to purport Chief Darryl Gates as a reason for this riot and aired South Central denizens' complaints that he didn't respond in time to the incipient crimes, resulting in city-wide destruction. Chief Gates responded that he had his men escort firemen to overwhelming call-in and that he did not want to send full forces into the area at first as it could create an agressive cross-fire between cops and robbers, resulting in potentially more casalties. (My paraphrasing.) It is a small miracle that no L.A.P.D. officers were killed in this riot and few deaths occurred at the hands of police and then only when fired upon first. The word "restraint" was the order of the night by these brave men.

    These deft tactics of Chief Gates managed to save his men as well as protect city firemen contain over 5500 conflagrations city-wide, not to mention innocent civilans who were spared in potential gun-fire. As far as the looting, I'm thankful nobody was killed over a C-D player or roll of toilet paper. Review the statistics.

                    Sincerely yours,

                    Julia Wells (CLINCH)

cc: Chief Darryl Gates

Letter to Chief Gates and LA Times

LOS ANGELES POLICE DEPARTMENT

DARYL F. GATES
Chief of Police

TOM BRADLEY
Mayor

P. O. Box 30158
Los Angeles, Calif. 90030
Telephone:

(213) 485-3202
Ref#:   1.1

May 22, 1992

Ms. Julia Wells
8456 Blackburn Avenue #7
Los Angeles, CA 90048

Dear Ms. Wells:

Thank you for your very kind, very uplifting letter of support.
In these very difficult times, Los Angeles Police Officers are
physically tired and emotionally drained. Receiving your letter
made a great difference, as it provided a light, positive moment
in the day.

The civil unrest in Los Angeles was a tragic event. The officers
have been surrounded by anger, fear, and a sense of loss on the
part of thousands of citizens. Receiving your letter provided a
fresh insight and a new perspective on the situation. Hopefully,
with the help of concerned, active citizens, we can rebuild this
City's pride and property. From the heart, I thank you.

Very truly yours,

DARYL F. GATES
Chief of Police

Chief Gates letter to me: L.A. riots

• • •

On 7 June 1992, Martin sent a letter in response to the L.A. riots:
He apologized for not writing in a while. Family problems had happened; his mother had broken her hip. He explained that writing is something he does for a living so it was hard for him to write letters—it's something he just did. He'd meant to call me during the riots but by the time when he finished his writing for the day in London, it was not a good time to call L.A. when I had probably just gotten into dreaming sleep.

He was worried about me during the riots, and was even more so when he had read the copy of my letter to LAPD Chief Daryl Gates I'd sent him. He remarked that the riots weren't self-contained like the L.A. Watts riots were, and had gotten close to my apartment. He asked me what I meant by "loaded up?" Did I mean my car… or my gun?

Martin called the marauders outside my window "designer rioters" from the way I described the gang of looters in my letter. He had read the riots were more of a class war than a race war, and wondered what South-Central (L.A.'s black inner city area) looked like now? He wanted to know what I would have done as my last resort? (Good question: if I hadn't escaped from my apartment, I definitely would have held my ground with my semiautomatic.)

Martin wrote he'd started a new novel about two authors (assumingly, this was *The Information*—that critics would later suggest was a disguised analogy of Martin and Julian Barnes). Also, he was being screwed around on a film script, but that a trip to L.A. was possible, and told me to read *The New Yorker* next month, which included his short story that took place in my town—L.A.

He had just finished a long essay on *Lolita*, which would be in the September issue of *The Atlantic*, and suggested reading *Lolita* for my Great Books Discussion group at the Beverly Hills Library. People told him he reminded them how bad Lolita's seducer was; Humbert Humbert— the pedophile who paid preteen Lolita to fondle him under his desk while he ogled her blonde girlfriend in his classroom. Humbert liked going down on the very languid "nymphet" (a term Nabokov coined for pubescent girls) when she had a fever because she coughed and shivered in his embrace. (Yikes, Humbert was creepy.) Martin closed with warm wishes and for me to stay well—love, Martin.

• • •

29 June 1992

Dear Martin,

I hope your mother's hip has improved since her fall, and all I can say for Sally is how hard life must be for some woman—unbearable—so they have to drink. I hope she can pull herself out of it. What kind of rut are you in? Old French? Or M.E.? There are 2 definitions in the dictionary.

In my last letter you asked what I meant when I "loaded up" in the L.A. riot. Well, all of us wild West Americans are "packin' heat" and have a pistol close at hand. (There is the term, "loaded" as drunk, but that was not an option; at least, not for me.) As for packin' heat, even the guy I recently went to dinner with carried a .38 automatic weapon into the restaurant and left the gun under the table! The busboy came running after us with a brown paper bag in his hands and returned it. (Isn't that what Robert Blake claimed had happened when his wife was shot in the car? The jury believed him and Blake was acquitted of murder.)

To answer your query about my "plan of last resort," I was prepared to rent a car and drive to Phoenix at my brother in law's advice when he called. His wife lives in Paris six months a year so he was alone. I later told him that even though L.A. was burning and under siege, I felt safer here! (Just kidding…in a way.) I also considered driving to Laguna Beach to my half-brother's house but the freeways were frozen in traffic, and LAX was shutdown. I thought about making a leap to Elaine's house in Beverly Hills, less than a mile away, but instead decided to stand my ground in the apartment with my semi-automatic—that's when I "loaded up."

When I opened your letter, I glanced at the back page at first, which read, 'He also enjoyed going down on her when she had a fever, etc.' I instantly flashed, *who* is he talking about? Sir K?! I turned the letter over and read the first page, and realized the quote was from Nabokov's *Lolita*, describing Humbert Humbert, dirty old man extraordinaire! Wasn't James Mason simply the best D.O.M ever in Stanley's Kubrick eponymous film?

Warm wishes,
Julie

• • •

P ost script: When I called the L.A.P.D. to ask if Chief Gates got my message immediately after the four police were found "Not Guilty," that is, didn't they anticipate turbulence from the African American community? I was a told, "We hope not." After the riots, Chief Gates was asked why was he on his way to a meeting in Brentwood in West L.A. when the verdict was read? He admitted, "It was dumb." I respected Chief Gates and considered him very intelligent (he got the highest scores on all the LAPD examinations) and he was kind (Chief Gates knelt down and petted Stormy, my Pekingese, during a support campaign I had attended.) Chief Gates had integrity and backed his officers in the department; while he acknowledged there were a few bad cops. There always are—in any group, but the buck stopped with him.

• • •

2 August 1992, a London postcard was in an envelope addressed to my apartment on Blackburn Ave, LA, CA.

Martin had handwritten that my letter made the riots terrifyingly vivid to him. And it reminded him that the things he only reads about actually happen. He asked if I had gone into shock afterward. He shared he did after he had experienced post-traumatic stress when he was forced to exit a commercial plane by sliding down a chute in an emergency landing. Martin wrote about his frightening ordeal in his nonfiction collection, *Visiting Mrs. Nabokov.*

He closed saying he was going to Cape Cod again on the New England peninsula, and while there, he planned to visit Saul Bellow in Vermont (more about that visit later.) He promised to report when he returned at the end of summer.

• • •

My Letters: Los Angeles -- London

12 October 1992

Dear Martin,

I've been reading your dad's *Difficulties with Girls* and wonder what Patrick meant when he said he "really did like Americans—REAL Americans." Does that mean the Sioux and Apache? And are all his male characters priapic? Or the antithesis? Really, I am really enjoying it.

I read your essay, "Lolita Remembered," in *The Atlantic* in September and liked your unique perspective on Nabokov's story of a middle-aged pedophile and his willing, pubescent victim. Bravo. Also I bought *The New Yorker* to read your short story. Its cover was something I related to; the subject, Hollywood, is like watching a movie I'm living in. I am both amazed and amused by the town. The story gave chuckles, but it's a bit too close for comfort.

Best wishes,
Love, Julie

• • •

In November 1992 Martin wrote back thanking me for my letter. As for being a correspondent, he mused why was it writers don't seem to write letters? (His literary idol, Nabokov, did. I have an edition of one book of his collected letters). Martin mentioned the recently published, *The Collected Letters of Philip Larkin* in UK, and reiterated why writers don't write letters anymore. The reviewers had been harsh about Larkin's private thoughts; they were very critical, considering people write their grumbles in letters that they may think at the time, but not necessarily believe. He prophesied books like "The Collected Faxes of ___" would be published in the future. (Note: In a few years this prediction would be obsolete with the technological leap in personal communications: emails, texts, social media, etc.)

Martin said he liked the excerpt of a story I had written and sent him, but he wouldn't compare me to any of three female characters; however, he did point out one phrase: "She never fooled a soul…or a man," as my distinctive style.

Martin was going to America for a week on the East Coast for a reading. He wouldn't make it to the West Coast on this trip, but maybe soon because he was interrupting his current novel by taking on the difficult task of rewriting *Mars Attacks* (the sci-fi comedy starring Jack Nicholson and Glenn Close as the U.S. President and first lady).

He wished me well and sounded on top of my game—that I even managed to write letters. On the other hand, he felt exhausted.

• • •

Eighteen

BACK TO THE HOMETOWN

One afternoon, under a hazy, yellow L.A. sky, I was lying on my sofa in my West Hollywood apartment looking across the boulevard at the Beverly Center, the imposing high-rise, a shopping beacon for consumers. A year had passed since from the same window I had watched well-clad looters running to smash windows and rob the luxury mall Mecca minutes before the LAPD and L.A. Sheriff deputies had dozens detained on their knees, elbows akimbo on their heads, and arrested them. Today I saw that public activity on La Cienega Blvd was business as usual, moving along in everyday traffic in the ordinary hurry of city life. My life in Los Angeles had reached its expiration date of twenty years. It was time to return to the small town I had grown up in, the home where my aging mother lived and needed me. I gave a thirty-day notice to my Israeli landlord and made arrangements with a moving company to deliver what little furniture I had, my books and clothes to Washington State. I bought a one-way ticket to SeaTac, packed two large suitcases, and took my beloved Pekingese, Stormy, on the plane with me as a carry-on.

On the flight from LAX to Seattle, I sat with Stormy snuggled inside his doggie kennel under the seat in front of me. I knew life would change dramatically, going from living in a large, metropolitan city to a small town, but I was ready for the pivotal life change ahead. My mother was living alone with her dog, Sasha, a Lhasa Apso, and sounded relived I was coming back to live with her now that she was almost eighty. Mom was getting more forgetful, not paying the monthly utility bills or property taxes on her house, which needed repairs and cleaning. Also because her new 'friend,' George, an eighty-two year old coot with limited common sense, was making daily, uninvited visits to her house, and she needed help in dealing with him "taking over."

Shortly after the initial acclimation to migrating back home, I joined a Great Books discussion group in Seattle and a local astronomy club. I got a job teaching yoga classes at Gold's Gym for two nights a week, and two for the city parks department. These activities got me out of the house, kept my mind stimulated, and my body fit.

Starting over in middle age is a challenge, but somehow life keeps moving, gets through the day, then the next week, and manages to move into the future. There's always something to do when you have a house to maintain, not to mention a mother who's losing her short-term memory. The relationships between mothers and daughters are known to be complicated; each seems to be difficult to the other. But now, mother was showing signs of progressive dementia and it became hard to be her sole caretaker; nevertheless, I felt an obligation. Mom made me promise when I was a girl that I would never put her in a nursing home when she became old, and she could live in her home as long as she wanted. I was determined to keep that promise.

Eventually a year passed since I had returned to my hometown. Slowly and steadily, I made the adjustment to living in prosaic, predictable, small-town America. The business of shopping for food and supplies, paying bills, cleaning house, home repairs, et cetera, kept me busy; also teaching yoga classes and walking daily with my dog, Wolfie—a 115 pound German Shepherd I had adopted from the local animal shelter—to the downtown library and used bookstores, while our small dogs, Stormy and Sasha, stayed home with mom to keep her company.

• • •

Nineteen

AUGUST 25, 1993

Private musings sent in the mail to Martin on his birthday. When the following letter arrived in London, Martin called me.

• • •

25 August 1993. It's Martin's birthday today. He's 44 years old. He must be with his family (wife and boys) in Cape Cod, Massachusetts, where they spend their annual summer vacation at his wife's family home. They don't return to London until after Labor Day, so he might still be there for his birthday.

I haven't heard from Martin since we spoke on the phone on April 1. His son was sick with whooping cough on top of asthma. I hope he's cured by now although Martin was very worried at the time. He sounded cooler in his voice inflection; he had a lot on his mind.

As for my mind, I'm trying to control my temper and mood swings, especially during PMS week every month. In the novel, *Other People, A Mystery Story*, [13] Martin wrote that even if a woman knows she's crazy for five days every month, it doesn't do her any good because she's crazy!

---

13 Martin Amis. *Other People: A Mystery Story*. London: Jonathan Cape, Inc., 1980

So how can I expect to control myself when I'm crazy? Doesn't crazy mean you have no control? I forget to apply this logic when people who are either crazy or drunk upset me. I anguish over their hurtful words because I forget that they're crazy! All we can do is try to remember they're not in their right mind, and to get away from them ASAP!

Hopefully I can take my own advice and stay away from crazy people until they've resolved their problems, and even avoid myself five days of the month with the help of "better living through chemistry" pharmaceuticals. (I envy people who can self-medicate with alcohol—a martini or two. I couldn't do that; I would only get a brief high with a long hangover.)

It's late and I've read a few more chapters in the Macintosh manual. When I am stuck on the Mac, the call-up tech always tells me to "RTFM!" (Read The F*****g Manual!) Now I'm going to smoke a 'rollie.' Martin showed me how to hand-roll cigarettes with Golden Virginia loose tobacco that he smoked. They are pretty good so I'm smoking while I will reflect on what I've just read. I like the Mac much better than the IBM computer I used in L.A., on which, incidentally, my entire work was lost because I didn't click 'Save.' I had spent the entire night writing on the subject of 'character'—what exactly was it? Is a person's character his true nature? Can you change your character? Martin had written, "Character is destiny." Does he mean this only about the literary characters he creates? Or does Martin believe people are born predisposed to have a good or bad character?

I remember Martin saying that a person remains the same from childhood into adulthood—even until they become old. Time goes by us, but we stay the same person throughout our lives. I told him that seemed discouraging because I'd like to think I have become a better person than when I was inexperienced, immature, and selfish. Martin admitted we could improve in many ways, but our true essence doesn't change. We can better ourselves—but we're still the same person we always were.

Visiting Martin Amis

Twenty-five years later, Martin Amis was quoted in an interview in *Vanity Fair* (Sept. 2012) *"Every 10 years you're a different person, and the really great books evolve with you as you get older"... "They're full of new rewards."* So what is it, Mart? Character vs. nature: are you saying our character can change, but not our true nature? I'm confused. It's a conundrum.

We have to work on a good character, per se. It's why people go to church, synagogue, mosque, temple, or follow a spiritual leader. It's a daily vigilance until doing the right thing becomes a habit. I believe most people want do the right thing, but they're so screwed-up in 'stinking thinking' that their decisions are often made by instant self-gratification and ego, with little thought about the moral consequences or other people. Meanwhile, my efforts are often futile because PMS brings an irrational week every month, come rain or shine. Then the vicious cycle begins over again. By the time Medusa rears her ugly head, I have forgotten the curse is imminent—and I'm going to be *less* than ladylike—and forget to 'chill with a pill.' Like Martin said, "You just have to ride it out."

• • •

A computer is a good place to be enlightened. It's like a psychic-selfie. Now it's August 27, 1993, and I have read two chapters of *The Rachel Papers*. I am appalled (no, that phrase has become a cliché). Better to say, I was dismayed, a more accurate description of my sensibilities when I read Martin's first novel. He was only twenty-three when he was writing this 'literature,' but it's still adolescent. (That age has to be some of the hardest years to go through, and many kids can't—and don't make it.)

Young Charles Highway in *The Rachel Papers* is not comparable with the protagonist teen, Holden Caulfield, in J.D. Salinger's *Catcher in the Rye*, although both can be called a Bildungsroman. In James Boswell's 19th Century journal, he may have had comparable, young man's reflections, but even if Boswell secretly explored a woman's undergarments two centuries earlier, he didn't *write* about it! James Boswell was a genius on another level.

Amis's Charles Highway doesn't compete with Salinger's Holden Caulfield or Boswell as young man; moreover, we're talking different eras and styles. But, for Amis to devote an entire chapter to panty exploration, and then go on to defile the poor girl in his dreams is described by a penciled-in, one-word review the city librarian wrote on the public library copy's title page—"Crap!"

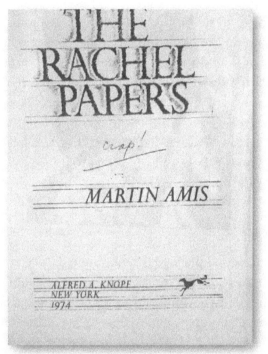

Library title page: The Rachel Papers

It's not that I ever thought Martin was infallible, but he's a reliable narrator. I often forget that boys tend to be vulgar and coarse in their thoughts about girls. It's a man's world, *nolo contendere,* so be it! At least Martin was young when he wrote *The Rachel Papers,* and he may even regret some of his earlier writings, as he confessed to me that he cringed at his former juvenile self—ye gods, haven't we all? I thought his piece, *My Oxford,* was superb and showed even in the beginning his writing style showed excellence. I wish I could find the entire work to read. The epiphany in *Other People, A Mystery Story* was that Mary read a lot because there was order in literature, as opposed to reality. That must be why I read so much; you can count on a story to 'un-confuse' you—at least, for a little while.

Martin's girl problems seem to have been greatly reduced, if not matured, a mere two novels after *The Rachel Papers,* and by a few years of experience with the tender sex. When some men get older, they become spiteful and bitter toward women; Martin seemed to like women more, but he did admit that a man wants to adore and defile a woman he loves—at the same time. That might have something to do with the Madonna-whore complex. Again, his polarity complex factors in.

When my mother saw the VCR tapes I recorded of Martin's interview with Charlie Rose, and Melvyn Bragg in Britain, she commented Martin seemed content in London. Why not? He has everything a man ought to have at middle age: success, wealth, family, health, and friends. It's only logical to assume he's satisfied. Again, the quote from John Lennon about people, "What you see is what it's not" caused me to think not.

In any case, I wish we could be friends, although James Joyce wrote that platonic love is not possible between a man and a woman. That's what Joyce implied in a short story I read when I was thirteen and have believed ever since. The problem goes back to the nature of both beasts. I wish it were possible because I really don't want anything else.

Martin once told me marriage and children were what one does at a certain time in life. It's what you do *next.* It was not my destiny—not in my stars. I've come to accept fate and am relieved I don't have to go through adolescence again in the form of a son or daughter's struggles. I still can't drive past my old junior high school without reflecting on those awful years.

I know my place is here taking care of with my mother in the house I grew up in, and our dogs. That's fine with me because I love them. Meanwhile life continues to be a challenge—a euphemism for extremely difficult, i.e., frustrating, and often overwhelming. Close for now.

• • •

Julia Clinch

It is several weeks later. Life has become a bit more stable as I've acclimated to this new environment on the Puget Sound in the Pacific Northwest. I was trying at first to bring order into a chaotic new place (my mother's house) and at the same time, synchronize with the new world into which I had suddenly whirled myself.

The disorder upended in my own life was compounded by the three-ring circus my mother was living in. Her house was filled with objects, collectables, and stuff my mother had hoarded and compiled—in some rooms, to the ceiling—in the past thirty years of my absence. Since her last boyfriend died (not George, he is still very much alive), Mom has lived alone with her dog, Sasha. But she was never lonely. Mother has her friends and cousins dropping by regularly—the front doorbell frequently rings without notice. When it does, I go into my bedroom and work on my computer. After all, this is her house and I'm happy to help her, even though it's made a tumultuous impact on my organized person—in addition to my migration north.

Mother's house has two floors and the upstairs filled to the brim with stuff mother has crowded into every conceivable square inch. She made a path to the carved, four-poster bed in which I was supposed to sleep; but, because of my claustrophobia, I did not even attempt to climb over piles of stuff in the stairwell to the room where it was located—under more stuff. Instead, I chose a downstairs bedroom, directly across the hall from her room, that I redecorated after clearing out the clutter. There was quite a bit of arguing about eliminating the vast amount of junk; finally, and dutifully, I conceded (most of it) to her domain. Again, I just wanted some order in the world so I could think straight.

This was her world I had come back to, so I relented, albeit, not always patiently; but it's hard taking care of a progressively forgetful parent. Just try it if you think I exaggerate. I want to be respectful to my mother and to acclimate in her home. Now my days are spent teaching yoga, cleaning, walking the dogs, going to the library, working on the computer, and hours upon hours of sorting and sneaking out endless boxes of junk.

Twenty

*"Award Winning novelist, Martin Amis, 44, whose
books include Time's Arrow (1991) and London Fields
(1989) has, according to British papers, separated
from his wife of nine years, Antonia, a writer."*

—PASSAGES, *PEOPLE MAGAZINE*, SEPT 27, 1993

Oh. My. God. NEWS FLASH! During the last entry my cousin, Jeff called
and said "GUESS WHO'S GETTING A DIVORCE?" He then exclaimed,
"MARTIN AMIS!" Jeff told me his sister, Kathleen, had read the news this
morning in *People* magazine. It blew my mind and I still haven't grasped it.

I was chatting online when Jeff called and told me that a notice in
People magazine reported that British author, Martin Amis had left his
wife in London. After thanking Jeff for the news flash, I dove into a pair
of jeans and ran to a nearby convenience store to buy September 27th
issue of *People* to see the news for myself. Shuffling to page 57, "Passages,"
I read that Martin Amis had separated from his wife, Antonia. I hurried
back home and immediately dialed Martin's phone number in London to
tell him that the news of his split had been published in *People* magazine.

Astonished, Martin said, "Really? Already?" I read him the text and
he said it was mistaken about his wife: "No, she's not a writer." But he

verified the separation was true. I asked him if he had met another woman, and he admitted that he that had.

"It doesn't surprise me you would leave your wife, but it does shock me you'd leave your boys. I mean, your dad did that to your mum and you. You were the same age as they are now."

"Yeah, I know." He sighed.

"I'm not surprised because it just seemed too pat—your marriage, I mean. Does that word translate trans-Atlantic-ally?"

He replied, "Yes, it does."

Martin told me his marriage had been smoldering for a while, and during this last summer, things blew up. It reminded me of his story, "Insight at Flame Lake"—an explosion had taken place near a body of water. Did both his "Flame Lake" and marriage break-up happen in Cape Cod, where Martin said his story idea came to him and where the Amises spent every summer at his in-laws. If so, then Martin's fiction and nonfiction reality had collided.

"Is she American?"

Martin said, "Yes."

"How old is she?"

"I don't want to talk about it. It's been very stressful right now."

"I understand," I said, and then wished him well before we said goodbye.

I immediately made plans to fly to England. I booked a reservation in West London at the Pembridge Court, a cozy little hotel in Notting Hill I found on the Internet, which, according to the map of London, was walking distance to Martin's writing studio. I was intent to do more research. I arranged for Jeff's sister, Kathleen, to come over during the day to make sure Mom and our dogs were taken care of while I was in London. I only planned to stay a week. Mother was still functioning satisfactorily on a limited basis; our neighbors were reliable, so Mom would be watched and could call them until I returned.

I mailed Martin a note that I was coming to London and, in tiny font print: "Don't do anything until I get there." I'm sure he grinned when he read it (as if I had anything to say about things.)

The cliché truth is stranger than fiction proved true again. I thought these things only happen in novels because people usually play it safer in life, but I was wrong! As Martin wrote in "Insight at Flame Lake," *Reality Is Out Of Control!* Plus, it's the most interesting part of life; just when you think you know what's going to happen, the unpredictable pops up and pulls the rug out from under you. We're never completely in control of life. This reality keeps one on his/her toes. Author, M. Scott Peck explained, "Reality is what you attend to." (You still can't control it.) He added whatever it is you attend to—a person, child, pet, job, money, yourself; that is your true love.

This younger woman was what Martin needed: romantic love and passionate sex, considering both had apparently paled in his marriage. Romantic sex usually doesn't stay exciting (or romantic) after years of everyday reality—especially after kids rear their little heads; at least, not until they grow up and leave the house.

In *London Fields,* Guy Clinch's wife, Hope, may have been based on Martin's first American wife. To wit, in his essay, "Lolita Reconsidered" — *The Atlantic Monthly* Sept. 1992, Martin wrote, *"A husband, too, can on occasion find his wife a little wearing particularly if she is a self-constructed simulacrum of the perfect American homemaker (all poise and know-how)... "*

Did Martin's way out of a tired marriage come by an exciting (older) "nymphet," (Nabokov's term) who was also American? According to "Famous Amis" by Michael Shnaynerson (*Vanity Fair,* May 1995) sources claimed Isabel Fonseca's moniker was "Isabel Fun-seeker" in London social circles. Rumor, Isabel was reputed to be a fun-seeking flirt—with her eye on writers and artists—allegedly, Salmon Rushdie and John Malkovich.

I was indeed surprised that Martin would leave his boys like his own father had left him and his siblings when they were the same ages. Now history was repeating itself in his adult life and he was leaving *his* family. But when you're in a loveless marriage, more often than not, kids aren't going to save it. I had sensed Martin wasn't happy with his marriage, but I never inquired. Even though we had intimate conversations in his book tours in Los Angeles, I didn't feel it was my place to ask questions about his family. John Lennon sagely noted, "What you see is what it's not"—implying all is not hunky-dory in other people's lives. To wit, I am not the proverbial temptress. Instinctively, I would not go beyond the Rubicon. People have a moral code to live by, but ardent passion often transgresses the parameters of one's moral compass.

• • •

My plane flew nonstop from Seattle to London. I took the train into West London, and checked into the Pembridge Court Hotel. It was late afternoon, but I was determined to see Martin. I showered, put on a fresh dress, and walked several blocks to his writing flat on Leamington Road Villas. When he opened the door, Martin didn't seem surprised to see me. I'm not sure if I had told him my arrival date, but he was very polite during my unexpected drop in and made coffee we took to drink the living room.

Martin in his studio kitchen

Martin signed his father's novel, *Jake's Thing*, I had brought: "My Dad's Thing—Martin Amis." I took photos of us together with my disposable camera. (The close-up shots made us *both* look like space aliens. Those old disposable cameras didn't have the efficacy of today's cell phones.) We talked about the new woman in his life, for whom he was leaving his wife. Martin said he'd been a friend of her brother's, Milo, and that she had also gone to Oxford. He was advising Isabel on a book she was writing about eastern European gypsies. (Isabel's father was a Uruguayan sculptor and she is the granddaughter of the late financier and philanthropists, Jacob and Alice Kaplan who were patrons of the arts in Manhattan. Her American family resides in New York City and in East Hampton, Long Island.)

Martin told me he was planning to marry her; I wished him much happiness. One could say Martin had the classic trappings of a man in midlife crisis: leaving his first wife and family for a younger woman; firing his longtime literary agent and signing with one in New York City. All he needed to do now was to buy a new, red sports car. Instead, Martin opted to have dental work done with oral implants for his teeth and gums that had pained him all his life—major life changes. Twenty years hence, Martin and Isabel are still married with two young daughters. Isabel wrote a novel, *Attachment*, about a distressed wife who suspects her husband is having an affair. (Years ago, there was a rumor alleging Martin had been with a Brazilian supermodel. Who knows? What goes around comes...etc.) The novel is fiction, but it could be a simulacrum of marriage. The old adage, write what you know.

Martin's second marriage was like the déjà vu plot of his first novel, *The Rachel Papers*: an Englishman falls in love with an American heiress—Rachel, assumedly, Jewish.

Meanwhile I was still booked at the Pembridge Court hotel for another seven nights, and my flight home wasn't scheduled until the following week. Throughout this seven-day interval, I again explored London nonstop, starting with an enormous English breakfast at the Pembridge Court. I didn't eat for the rest of the day, except for an egg sandwich that I made with a hard-boiled egg and toast from breakfast, or once or twice, a hot pub dinner. Consequently, continuous walking around London my body weight dropped to 105 pounds. (After I got home, a neighbor woman said my head looked too big for my body. Nice.) I rode the Tube to London's historical sites I hadn't seen before, this time to its outer-zone areas where I got out and walked around a Middle Eastern neighborhood. All the women wore *hijabs* and black *burkas*; the ethnic shops and markets were posted in Arabic. I was the only non-Muslim as far as I could see and was clearly out of place; I took the next bus back to central London. In the afternoon, I went to a matinee performance in the Theatre District and shopped for quaint souvenirs at the outside stands on Portobello Road—a block around the corner from my hotel.

A band from America was also staying at the perfectly located Pembridge Court—singer, Lenny Kravatz. He was standing at the front desk when he heard my American accent, and asked where I was from. I told him Seattle and Kravatz said it was where his idol, Jimmy Hendricks, was born and buried. Lenny was very nice; he gave me a CD of his new album.

One day, having combed through London, I decided to take the train to Oxford University, an hour outside the city. A top university in the world, Oxford University was famous for its outstanding curriculum in education. As famous as its counterpart, Cambridge University, Oxford's renowned professors and brilliant dons graduated genius physicists, philosophers, authors, and scientists for centuries; while Cambridge had titans like Sir Isaac Newton and Stephen Hawking to grace their physics chair. Today I had the opportunity to visit Oxford University, the alma mater of Martin Amis and his father, Kingsley Amis. (Martin had gotten highest marks from its Exeter College.)

I walked from the station to the Oxford campus and toured its extended grounds and mustard-colored, old buildings of its several colleges. An unassuming entrance stood in the middle of a building marked the Bodleian Library. I entered the small lobby of the famous library, knowing it contained invaluable manuscripts and literary masterpieces from millennia. Luminaries, scientists, and learned men and women came to research and to read its irreplaceable trove. Major advances and discoveries in the natural sciences, ancient Roman law, medieval and handwritten history, and original editions of English literature are stored under hermetic seals.

My visit to the Bodleian Library in Oxford reminded me of an incident that Martin wrote about when he and his new family visited the Dome of the Rock in Jerusalem, Israel. I found it compared ironically with my experience at the door of the Bodleian—specifically, Martin's reaction on being turned away at the exhibition of the Dome of the Rock.

In the long essay, "Terror and Boredom" in *The Second Plane: September 11,* Martin wrote:

> There exists on our planet a kind of human being who will become a Muslim in order to pursue suicide-mass murder. I will never forget the look on the gatekeeper's face at the Dome of the Rock in Jerusalem when I suggested, perhaps rather airily, that he skip some calendric prohibition, and let me in anyway. His expression, previously cordial and cold, became a mask, and the mask was saying that killing me, my wife, and my children was something for which he now had warrant. — Martin Amis, *The Second Plane: September 11*, New York: Alfred A. Knopf (2008).

When I was at the door of the Bodleian Library, the elderly doorman informed me the library was temporarily closed and wouldn't reopen until later that day. Like Martin, I "airily" suggested that he overlook the temporary injunction and let me in anyway. The look on his face was tantamount to "Are you nuts, or are you simply a moron?" His instant disdain for asking him to break the rules seemed he overreacted to my naïve, and airheaded request. However, I did not for one second think he wanted to kill me (or my family—had I one) as Martin interpreted his parallel encounter at the Dome of the Rock. Critics alleged that Martin was oversensitive, taking offense from the Moslem gatekeeper because his wife and daughters were Jewish. To be fair, both doormen—in Jerusalem and in Oxford—were just doing their job; but Martin took the incident personally—as a threat to himself and his family. [14]

After my energy was spent all afternoon touring the historical environs of Western education at Oxford University, I walked back to the town train station and boarded the next train to London. On the way, the train stopped at a small town where many of the passengers got off to have a drink at the station cafe. Seated next to my table was a young woman having a cup of tea. We exchanged a few pleasantries, and introduced ourselves. Myra Lansing told me she was a twenty-nine-year-old lawyer who worked in a legal office in Westminster, the judicial area of London. We struck up a conversation that continued as we re-boarded the train and sat next to each other on the way back to London.

Myra asked why I was in London, so I told her I was visiting my writer friend, Martin Amis. Myra was delighted to hear this and showed a keen interest in how I'd gotten to know the English author and the interview he had given me. Myra was knowledgeable about popular culture and the aspects of Martin's current life from reading the many London newspapers and tabloids she bought every day at corner news kiosks on the way home from her office in Westminster to her London flat. She seemed eager to hear intimate information about Martin firsthand and asked a lot of questions. Traveling alone thus far as a foreigner in England, I was delighted to have a new acquaintance.

Arriving at Paddington Station in London that evening, we were still engaged in lively conversation. By this time we were both hungry and agreed to have dinner together before parting for the night. With an

---

14 Jonathan Tepperman wrote about Amis' comment: "This isn't satire, or keen observation. It's just bile." Stranger Than Fiction, Books: *Newsweek* April 14, 2008. – Jonathan Tepperman. "Martin Amis: I, Crackpot?" http://www.newsweek.com/martin-amis-i-crackpot-86021

education in law, Myra was an interesting young woman with whom I felt we could be friends. After a hearty dinner of English stew at a pub we found nearby, we exchanged home phone numbers. I gave Myra my address in the States and promised to stay in touch. As we shook hands goodbye, I hoped to see Myra again.

I saw Martin once more before leaving London and returning to America and back home. He was determined to marry Isabel. Again I wished him the best and meant it.

Not long after I arrived home, the shit hit the London press-fan over Martin's recent advance of £500,000 (British pounds) for his new novel— *The Information* (1995), as well as his recent life changing actions. Not only did he leave his wife and young sons, but he also fired his London literary agent of twenty years for the New York agent, Andrew Wiley, who mediated the huge financial advance. To wit, Martin's latest novel was notable for its critical success, but also for the scandal surrounding its publication. Scandal is a great expedient for publicity—"Just spell my name right."

The unheard-of-book advance demanded and subsequently obtained for Amis by his new agent attracted what Martin described as "an *eisteddfod* of hostility" from other writers and critics. Literary circles censured Amis for abandoning his long-serving literary agent (the late) Pat Kavanagh to sign with the Harvard-grad, Andrew Wylie in New York. The split was contentious; it created a rift between Amis and his best friend, Julian Barnes, who was married to Kavanagh. According to Martin's memoir, *Experience* (2000), he and Barnes still had not resolved their differences. Critics and readers speculated that *The Information*—the story of a rivalry between two British novelists—was based on his relationship with Barnes; for the record, Amis has denied this.

Myra sent me several news clippings from London newspapers that sensationalized the brouhaha of Martin Amis's large book advance, brokered by his new agent. British literary circles decried Martin Amis as greedy and thoughtless toward his fellow writers. On January 5, 1995, The *Evening Standard* published in block-letter headlines, "Martin Amis attacked in £500,000 'greed' row'."[15] The article reported, "Open warfare erupted among Britain's literary establishment today as Booker Prize winner, A.S. Byatt criticized fellow novelist Martin Amis for 'macho posturing' over his demand for a £500,000 advance." Writers and critics joined Byatt en masse in a bitter rebuke of Amis in both London's daily press and in its literary salons.

Gossip flew like geese across London's social and private club circles, as the press fed off the enticing roast of the famous novelist. London tabloids had a month long field day over Amis abandoning his London family and leaving his longtime literary agent, Pat Kavanagh, to sign with Andrew Wylie. *The Daily Telegraph* [16] stated Kavanagh "is said to be hopping mad" about the author's decision to hire the New York agent, Andrew Wiley. The *Telegraph*'s bold headline, "Martin Amis goes the way of 'the Jackal'," parodied Andrew Wylie's nickname, the Jackal, the new agent who brokered the huge advance. Known for his tenacity, Wylie's list of writers included Salman Rushdie, V. S. Nepal, William Burroughs, Ben Okri, Germaine Greer, and Martin's fiancée, Isabel Fonseca. *The Telegraph* went on to report that A.S. Byatt "denounced Amis for indulging in a kind of male turkey cocking, which is extremely bad for the industry and makes life hard for young authors."

London's *Evening Standard* went on to state Ms. Byatt was incensed over his huge financial coup, and she continued fuming, "Battles for huge advances in the sort obtained by Mr. Wiley usually led to sourness and subsequently very small advances and the knockoff effect damage the whole industry. "Byatt continued blasting Amis. "I always earn out my advances and I don't see why I should subsidize his greed, simply because he has a divorce to pay for and has just had all his teeth redone." (From the coffers of the unprecedented advance.) "Mr. Amis, 45, recently split from his wife, Antonia Phillips, now lives in New York with his American

---

15 Martin Delgado and Sandra LaVille. "Martin Attacked in £500,000 'greed row'." London: *Evening Standard*, 5 Jan 1995. Daily Newspaper. p. 3
16 Susannah Herbert. "Martin Amis goes the way of 'the Jackal.'" London: *The Daily Telegraph* 6 Jan 1995. Arts Correspondent. (*The Telegraph*) p. 5

girlfriend, Isabel Fonseca. She is said to have persuaded him to spend some £20,000 on dental work." [17]

Martin's career move incensed a slew of other English writers, including Martin's best friend (until then) author Julian Barnes, husband of Amis' former agent. Filled with animus, Barnes gave Amis a very personal bashing in the form of a letter. Barnes expressed his rebuke of Martin for leaving his family, Antonia and their two young boys, to run off with a younger woman. On a personal level, was the egregious betrayal of Martin dumping his agent, Barnes's wife, Pat Kavanagh, for "the Jackal" Wylie. The Barnes's had been Martin's closest friends for years, during which time Pat had worked diligently on Amis successful career. Reportedly, Barnes ended the letter with a resounding, "F*ck off."

After the bitter rejection from Julian Barnes, Martin later admitted in *Experience*, that he was severely affected by the loss of his best friend. Nevertheless, Barnes' censure did not deter Martin from his making the life changing decisions. He signed with his new agent, Andrew Wylie, married Isabel, and moved to New York.

By 1995, Martin and Isabel had left London and the relentless tattle of the media. Soon after, Isabel took Martin to a New York orthodontist to have his teeth replaced with dental implants. (Martin said this was due to his bad gums, which had troubled him all this life.) Isabel made the big decisions, Martin admitted, and he went along with them. It's not unusual for men to let their wives make the main decisions: where to live (e.g., Uruguay), what house to buy, children, etc., since men have more important things to attend.

Myra continued sending me articles on Martin's public woes from newspapers and tabloids she bought daily that kept me up to date on his professional and personal crises. The ignominious headlines spread schadenfreude to many London literati and were celebrated by his

---

17 Martin Delgado and Sandra LaVille. "Martin Attacked in £500,000 'greed row'." London: *Evening Standard* 5 Jan 1995. p. 3

detractors. London's writer parties served smorgasbords of just desserts, cheeky éclairs, and payback pie.

A lengthy profile of Martin, titled, "Famous Amis" [18] by Michael Schnayerson was feathered in *Vanity Fair* (May 1995). The contributing editor wrote, even though "Martin Amis has always been portrayed as deeply cool, emotionally detached, cynical... But the person whom I spent time with was quite shaken and emotionally vulnerable." [19]

• • •

---

18 "Famous Amis," by Michael Shnayerson, an in-depth piece on Martin Amis, reported, "According to a close friend, that Isabel, the younger woman Martin was seeing while he was married to his first wife, Antonia, visited and had tea her with as she tearfully lamented her marriage was falling apart. Little did Antonia know that between these tea talks, Isabel was sleeping with her husband." - *Vanity Fair,* May 1995. pp. 132-162.
19 Michael Shaynerson. Ibid. *Vanity Fair* May 1995. Contributors. p. 20

Twenty-One

LIVING WITH MOTHER

My mother has a 'friend' named George Whitehall who is 82 or 84 (it varies whenever he tells it) and he plans to live to 102. George comes over every day and proposes marriage to my mother who politely turns him down. He's years older than my mom and I wonder sometimes if he is literate. I often wonder how people like him manage to survive, but they do and we both believe he will, although his son died in a car crash at twenty-five. No surprise there. George has never had any culture, except from the backwoods west of the Cascade Mountains where rednecks drink every night until the booze is gone, and meth labs are the town industry. He doesn't have a lick of common sense either, but he is sometimes useful, for instance, to send to the store for something we're out of. He's a widower and his neighbors, who are good friends of my mom, said when his wife was alive, never heard George and her exchange a word—that should give you a clue right there.

Whenever we 'take a drive' to his old stomping grounds about fifty miles into a Washington forest he shows us where dead bodies used to be found, and still are in the thick woods not far from the roads less traveled. George will tell us about his old cronies who had names like "Matt Starwick" and "Luke May." Even I had to appreciate names like these and could only imagine what they were like. I drive, mind you, because George has Parkinson's disease, which doesn't stop him from driving himself although his doctor told him not to. By the way, George is "stone deaf," (mom's words) without his hearing aid, which he doesn't like to wear. I drive his car, a Ford Thunderbird, to the mountain areas where we pull in and have a bite at a local, family cafe or truck stop. Once I happen to reach under the driver seat and found a fully loaded, 6 round revolver that I quickly pulled out and demanded to know "what the hell?" George told me to put it back under the seat where he kept it "for self-defense."

There are a few hair-raising stories I could tell you about George like the time he shot off a BB gun in our living room. I was doing a yoga headstand at the time and my cousin Oz said must've been 'a holler' because my legs were up in the air at the time of the gunshot. Another time George started an electrical fire fooling around with an obsolete lamp fixture. This is a typical hazard of living around the elderly. George smokes non-filtered Lucky Strike cigarettes, but thank goodness, he doesn't drink a lot. My mother likes to cook for him; it's her selfless, nurturer nature. One week he brought a jar of oysters every night for her to fry up. Every night.

New day, very close to D-D-day (Down in the Dumps) and I feel relatively all right. I mean, I'm my usual PMS depressed self, but not ultra emotional. I'm not dismally despondent—just hopeless. That may sound incongruent, but the fact my physical self got enough sleep last night and I'm reasonably healthy—from the neck down—is sufficient to keep me above the suicidal ideation threshold. The hopeless part comes from nothing to look forward to—just maintenance and survival. I'm keenly aware of being alive, and not wandering unconsciously through the day. I'm content to be in my hometown where I most likely will live until I reach "the big sleep" (homage to Raymond Chandler). This typical, small American town is mainly working class, resting on scenic Port Gardner Bay on the shores of Puget Sound in the Great Pacific Northwest. The landscape lies between the water and the mountains. If I were an outdoors person—e.g., sports, boating, biking, fishing, and hiking—it would be a perfect environment, but I'm not.

I have a lot to be grateful for: my mother and our dogs are well; I'm comfortable as far as living standards go. I don't need any material things, and when I view the current events down in L.A., I'm really relieved to be away from the mayhem and pandemonium of 'false idols.'

When my cousins teasingly asked me, "Why is it, Jules, you are always up here when Heidi Fleiss goes on trial in L.A.?" I told them I'm was in the Federal Witness Protection act, living incognito in my mom's home until the L.A. Madam, Heidi Fleiss scandal is resolved in the pending court trial. It was a joke to their teasing but a few believed it because, well, they wanted to. When they told 'Sinisister' the answer I gave them, she had to add her two cents, and snickered, "I hope Heidi Fleiss gives retirement benefits!" thinking her jab was clever, but it came off snide; the sarcasm negated any humor. Oscar Wilde she is not.

I am adamant not to read the Sylvia Plath piece in *The New Yorker* that came in the mail yesterday. My mood would plummet down, and the line I glanced from Robert Lowell that "life was not worth it" was enough for me to avoid the voluminous article. (Lowell was a lifelong manic-depressive, and was institutionalized more than once before Lithium was approved to treat his bipolar disorder. "And all because of a missing salt," he remarked when the drug mitigated the extremities of his symptoms.) Like it or not, I am "stuck with life," as Walter Clinch so prosaically informed me when I was twenty-two. I have to accept the ineffable phenomenon of being alive—one day at a time.

Twenty-Two

TRIP TO GERMANY AND LONDON

N ew romantic pastures to graze with a boyfriend I started dating after a recent high school reunion. Michael lived in Homer, Alaska, and owned a fishing boat that was very lucrative during salmon and halibut season. A long-distance love affair was on the horizon, and it was not that far away. Our first trip together was to a yoga retreat in the tiny village of Puerto Angel, Mexico, an hour south of Escondido in the Mexican state of Guadalupe. Michael had flown from Alaska to the Seattle airport, Sea-Tac, where I joined him on the plane to Mexico. I had purchased a round-trip ticket, paid my yoga and camping fees for some much needed R&R.

We flew into Mexico City, where we had a six-hour layover until the flight to Escondido. We never left the airport. That should tell you a lot about Michael. Was he afraid we'd miss the final leg of our connection and not catch the ground ride to Puerto Angel? I don't know, but I went along with him, as I often did with a boyfriend. Those who travel know that six hours in an airport is a long time. It wasn't until later, after other trips, like one to New Orleans (he paid for that), and some of his business decisions, that I learned his ideas were not very practical. Meanwhile, I thought I was "in love"—that oxytocin does it every time.

(**Oxytocin** is a hormone central to biological functions; especially specific to women, known as the "love hormone.")

After the yoga retreat in Mexico (which was fabulous on the beautiful beach in Port Angel), Michael flew down to see me frequently when fishing season was over. Once I drove with him from San Bernardino, California—where we'd flown down to pick up a car—up through Washington State through British Columbia and the Yukon Territory in Canada, to Homer, Alaska, in late November. All along the snow and icy trip, herds of caribou and moose wandered by the frosty roadside outside the car and scores of bald eagles perched on white-laden tree branches. I was still taking care of mother who by now had slipped further into dementia. I found a caretaker for her whenever Michael and I got together for a rendezvous. Our touch-and-go relationship was passionate and sometimes rocky. In spite of my volatile emotions, I was convinced I wanted to spend my golden years with him.

• • •

More than a year went by when it came time for Michael to leave for his annual Alaska fishing season—first for halibut and then for salmon—in Bristol Bay, Alaska. He'd fishing for three months, with little or no contact from his boat out on the open seas. I knew taking care of my mother without being able to contact him would make for a long, lonely summer.

In June I heard that my neighbor's daughter, Tory, was going to Germany to visit her sister, who was working at a U.S. Army base near Munich. I asked if I could go too, and Tory immediately said yes because she was going alone and had never been to Europe before. In two weeks we had our plane tickets and first-class passes for the *Deutsch Bahn*, German train.

We flew to Düsseldorf, Germany, where we checked into a hotel, then walked to the Old Town, the original quarter of the city. The next morning after we had caught up on our jet lag after the long flight, we boarded the *Deutsch Bahn* to Bonn and Cologne where we stayed over-night, then took the train south to Munich, where Tory's sister worked at the front desk of a Bavarian lake resort reserved for U.S. Army officers and their families near the capital. Hitler and his mistress, Eva Braun, and close friends would spend vacations at this lake resort before his fiftieth birthday when the Fuhrer was presented with *Kehlsteinhaus*, the Austrian mountain hideaway known as the Eagle's Nest (After Hitler would retreat and entertain dignitaries there.)

We stayed in Tory's sister and husband's studio in a building Hitler's laborers had built for German soldiers. Tory and I took several trips around the Bavarian region, notably to Ludwig II, the mad King of Bavaria's palace, and to the serene lake where he mysteriously disap-peared one night—rumor is he had been drowned amid his beloved swans. We rode the train to Strasbourg, Austria, and then to Füssen, a popular ski resort at the southern tip of Germany on the border of Switzerland. We toured two historic castles in the region, the spectacu-lar, fantasy-like Neuschwanstein Castle, named for King Ludwig's white swans. (Neuschwanstein Castle was the Disneyland model for Walt Disney's Fantasyland castle in Anaheim, California.)

My favorite excursion was a weeklong trip to Prague, the capital of the former nation of Czechoslovakia. Being jostled on train tracks all night in a sleeper car crossing into Czechoslovakia, I imagined being on the same train tracks that transported German Jews to Nazi concentra-tion camps. Customs officers woke us twice, once by German and then by Czechs, to secure our passports, which were returned when we reached the Prague station. (This had been required for all European countries before the European Union opened the borders.)

As soon as Tory and I arrived in Prague, we stood dismayed in its dilapidated train station that blazoned we were in the Third World. As we looked around the run-down station, a thin, young man dressed in a thread-worn shirt and mismatched pants approached us and offered a flat we could lease in Prague. We followed him to a tram outside the station and boarded it for a short ride to a stop across from an old apartment building where he told us to enter. Once inside, we climbed three, old stairways to a modest, but clean flat that shared a small foyer with to another flat. The room had two beds and a small kitchenette with a kerosene burner. We paid him for a week in advance and he left us the key. He told us to lock the door and leave the key under the mat when we left. We never saw him again.

Once settled in, we unpacked and took a quick sponge bath in the bathroom down the hall; then ventured outside to explore the medieval old city. After walking two miles on stone streets between centuries old, gray buildings, we climbed a steep hill that overlooked the City of a Hundred Spires (today Prague has over five hundred.) On top of the city's hill stood the majestic Byzantine castle where Slavic kings ruled Eastern Europe for eight hundred years in the Dark Ages. Prague is a unique city with barrages of baroque churches around its famous old town square and medieval astronomical clock, first installed in 1410, making it the world's oldest operating astronomical clock.

Crossing the fourteenth-century Charles Bridge on the Vltava River, we marveled at the sculpted statues of saints and glorious warrior angels that guarded the walkway over the river. The Charles Bridge is one of most outstanding sights in Eastern Europe. Walking randomly through the stone streets, we found ourselves at Prague's Museum of Modern Art and went inside. The Czechoslovakian paintings were dazzling with vivid colors and sensuality that stood out among the famous Impressionists along side those of Picasso, Degas, Monet, and Matisse.

When we returned to Munich on the Czechoslovakia and *Deutsch Bahn* train, Tory was bitten by wanderlust and wanted to go to Hungary to visit Budapest. By then, I opted to go to London and visit Myra, who had invited me to stay in her flat when she found out I was planning a trip to Germany. Tory's sister, Gretchen, drove me to the Munich airport on the Autobahn at ninety-five miles per hour. I am still amazed we arrived alive.

• • •

After a two hours flight, I landed at Gatwick Airport in London and called Myra at her solicitor office in a London judicial area. Myra told me to meet her on the corner outside her office building. I took a taxi to a section in Westminster, and waited on the sidewalk with my suitcase until Myra appeared from a towering, gray brick building.

I followed her into the building, up a winding, narrow, hardwood staircase to her tiny office—the size of a walk-in closet in which a desk, chair, and small filing cabinet were snuggled.

I sat in the little chair while Myra gathered up her legal papers and stuffed them into a briefcase. She grabbed her coat and purse and said to follow her downstairs. As we walked to the nearest Tube station, Myra began to tell me about an affair she was having with a lawyer in her office.

"He's married. They have two kids. He told me he's not leaving them anytime soon."

"Doesn't that concern you?" I asked.

"Not at all. In fact, I prefer that he's married. It makes things less complicated."

I was surprised to hear all this. Come to think of it, I knew very little about Myra, except that she was a solicitor (British term for lawyer) and lived alone in a one-bedroom flat in West London. She had sent me several letters and cards, mostly newspaper clippings about Martin Amis tattle, but suddenly I realized I didn't know anything about Myra herself.

"His name is Bob. We've kept our affair a secret. Nobody knows about it, except now you."

By now we were in the Underground tube and Myra had bought tickets to the Notting Hill Gate station. I didn't ask where we were going as I listened to her talk about her married lover, Bob. I assumed we would walk to her flat once we arrived at Notting Hill Gate. It didn't occur to me we were heading to a neighborhood near my cousin's house and Martin's writing flat.

"We've been having a love affair for over two years now." Myra eagerly informed me, "He comes over to my flat once a week, but I see him every day at the office, Monday through Friday."

"Doesn't it bother you that on holidays, Christmas, or vacations, he's with his family and not you?"

"No. Why should it?"

"It just seems to me that it would." I replied, nonplussed.

"Well, it doesn't. I like the arrangement we have."

I wanted to tell her, "I wouldn't want to share my lover living and sleeping with another woman," but I didn't.

Once the train reached Notting Hill Gate station, Myra hurried out the exit doors when I noticed she'd left her briefcase on the floor of the tube where we'd been sitting. I grabbed it and quickly caught up, handing it to her. "Myra, you forgot your briefcase."

She nonchalantly replied, "Oh, yeah," and took it without thanking me.

Obviously, her mind was on her torrid love affair. "You must have been thinking of B-o-b," I teased her.

"Like no one can tell who you're talking about." She chided me. I didn't reply to this jab, since no one was listening to her banter.

Myra walked around the corner to Pembridge Road, and I scurried along behind like a pet dog, until she stopped to hail a London taxi. As we rode several blocks this part of West London began to look familiar.

A little later the driver pulled over and we got out on Aldridge Road Villas. Myra paid the driver and we walked down the residential street until we came to a three-story, mustard colored building where Myra stopped,

"Here we are."

Now I had realized we were in the vicinity of Martin's writing flat on Leamington Villas Road, but I wasn't sure exactly where it was. I made a mental note to walk around the neighborhood at my earliest opportunity and look for it. I suspected an uncanny coincidence being near Martin's studio as noteworthy, but events were going by so quickly I didn't dwell on it by the time we climbed the stairs to Myra's third floor flat.

The most remarkable thing about Myra's apartment—or flat, as it's called in England—was that it looked like it had never been cleaned. Upon entering the room, I was amazed what a filthy pigpen the place was. I followed Myra around the living room, speechless as I stepped over piles of books, newspapers, and dishes with half-eaten food on them, plus crumbs and dust balls scattered on the floor. The salon carpet looked as if it had not been vacuumed in years, if ever. The kitchen was a little tidier although still messy, but the bathroom took the prize. It looked like she used the shower and brushed her teeth, but no other washing took place in this washroom.

Although it would take time getting used to, I was a guest in Myra's flat and she'd invited me, so I decided to make the most of the situation, which would only be for a few days. I just hoped I wouldn't catch anything from the house of grit and grime.

I continued to follow Myra around the flat as she chatted away about Bob. He definitely had her by the short and curlies. Personally, I didn't care if she had an affair with a married man. It was her life, and it was up to Myra to live it the way she wanted, even if she would most probably end up dejected and alone. Myra filled up a water-decanter from the kitchen faucet and told me to follow her down the outside stairs to the garden. Hers was a three-by-three-foot patch of soil allocated to each tenant on the interior yard of the building. I watched Myra water a few wilted flowers and plants. I'd always heard the British loved their English gardens and Myra was no exception.

Back in the flat, I was told to sleep on the sofa in the living room. As I got ready to go to bed, I attempted to clean up the sink in the bathroom as best I could before washing and brushing my teeth, but there were no cleaning supplies. It was a challenge with no washcloth or sponge, so I grabbed a wad of toilet paper and hand soap to wash down the facets and the filthy sink before I used them. I couldn't comprehend how anyone could live this way—in one's own compiled dirt. You couldn't tell by looking at Myra that she had household hygiene issues. Her clothing looked clean and ironed, her short brown hair was washed and combed, her complexion clear with light lipstick. Who would have guessed she lived in a pigsty?

The second surprise happened the next morning. It was a Saturday so Myra didn't have to go to work and had slept in. I had gotten up before her and had made instant coffee in the kitchen. Without any warning, Myra walked into the kitchen—stark naked.

Speechless, I stood aghast, staring at her, while she acted as if nothing was amiss and poured herself a cup of coffee. I managed to pull myself together and asked, "Aren't you afraid your neighbors across the street will see you standing naked in the window?"

She peered out the open velour blinds of her kitchen window and looked at the apartment building across the street. "I don't care if they can see me. It doesn't matter."

Myra had a slim, Anglo-Saxon white body, pristine enough to be a virgin's. The fact remained here was a totally nude woman in broad daylight standing in front of a third-story window that was open to public view. What could I say? After all, it was her home. Different strokes for different folks, or was she asking to be assaulted from a random neighbor or a sex fiend? Some might say yes. I doubt she was conscious of this; more likely, Myra's statement was her personal rebellion against social mores.

She was more than eager to talk about her assignations with her married, co-worker, Bob, and had convinced herself she was satisfied with the situation, per se. Even though he was had a wife and two children, she saw Bob weekly when he made his conjugal visits to her flat. To Myra, this was an ideal affair, even though the relationship was purely suited to his terms.

"I've never had an orgasm," she informed me out of the blue one afternoon.

"Bob has tried to give me one, but it's never happened to me."

"Why do you think you can't have one?" I asked, not really wanting to know.

"I don't know, but I like it when we have sex. Or at least he does." She added, "I like when he kisses and holds me in his arms."

Myra told me about her estranged relationship with her parents who lived north of London. She rarely saw them. She was an only child, and they had paid for her education and law degree at the university. For some reason she never made it clear why she didn't like them.

After we spent a day on errands Myra needed, I bought tickets for us to attend an outdoor production of Shakespeare's *The Tempest* in Hyde Park that evening. We took the Tube across town and found our seats in the last row of the park's amphitheater. It was a cold, windy night, interspersed with spattering of London's drizzling rain. Shivering, we sat high up in the bleachers and tried our best to keep warm snuggling in our wool coats.

"This weather is a perfect setting for *The Tempest*," I observed. We're practically in one

When Myra was busy on her legal work in the other room, I telephoned Martin at his writing flat in the vicinity and left a message to call me back on Myra's number.

Myra and I got along okay; although she was miffed I didn't want to go to Bath, in the ancient Britannica area founded by the Romans that had served as thermal baths for the Roman aristocracy—hence, its name. Bath was also the country home of Jane Austen, Britain's nineteenth-century literary treasure. I had already visited Bath on an earlier trip, having read Austen's novels. The Roman underground baths and saunas that Caesar's centurions had built were fascinating, but I was wanted to take in more sights in London I hadn't yet seen.

On Sunday, Myra planned a trip to Kew Gardens—the Royal Botanic Gardens that comprise 121 hectares of gardens and botanical glass-houses between Richmond and Kew in southwest London. She brought along Harriet, an older lady, who met us at a Tube station on route. Myra had packed a lunch in a wicker basket with plastic utensils and plates she bought especially for the afternoon picnic. It was very thoughtful of her, but all I could think was how Myra constantly complained, "I'm always out of money until my next salary." This never stopped her from buying everything she wanted including convenient snacks, teas, and a slew of tabloids and newspapers on her way to and from work.

I love to be among nature's bounty and beauty, especially flowers and trees, but even though it was sunny, it appeared to be off-season in Kew Gardens. We were in England's largest botanical gardens, but I didn't see any bloom of color, except for one small English rose. The botanical greenhouses offered a sample of every plant variety and floral species in the Commonwealth; but the outside gardens left something to be desired. It was midsummer, so perhaps the flowers had already lost their spring bloom.

Later on in the week I stopped by my cousin's house where a Pakistani businessman from Owen's bank was in his living room. He asked, "How did you like Kew Gardens?"

"It was very large with many garden paths to walk around. The greenhouses were, well, greenhouses with lots of botanical specimens; but frankly, the outside gardens looked like a bunch of weeds."

Owen and his associate laughed.

On Monday morning, Myra went back to work. This gave me the opportunity to explore the neighborhood. I got out a map of London and to my consternation, saw that Aldridge Road Villas was *one* block parallel to Leamington Road Villas: Martin's writing flat was on the very next street! He could be working on his old typewriter right now. In a rush of adrenalin, I quickly showered, pulled on my jeans, applied lipstick, threw on a top, and scurried down the stairs to the street — Aldridge Road Villas. I turned left and walked a short way to the corner; then turned left again on the corner of Leamington Road Villas when I looked up before my eyes to see Martin's flat where we had met and had spent hours together a decade ago.

Overcome by this incredible coincidence, I stared for a while at the second story of the old rectory in which we had the interviews. I imagined that Martin was typing on the "heapy, old thing," churning out another novel.

I decided not to cross the few yards of Leamington Road or enter the small courtyard and ring the upstairs doorbell. Instead, I walked back around to Myra's flat and dialed Martin's phone number. When his recorder answered, I left a message saying I was still at my friend's flat—and, was coincidentally, one block away—on Aldridge Road Villas. I added, since he hadn't returned my first call that I knew how Julian Barnes felt.

Martin did not call back, but he did bring up my voice recording a few years later in Oxford, Mississippi, where he confronted me about that message, in which he mistakenly heard me say I was Mrs. Julian Barnes.

• • •

Twenty-Three

JOURNAL 1999: IAN MCEWAN IN SEATTLE

I just came home from Elliott Bay Bookstore in Seattle where Ian McEwan read from his Booker Prize winning novel, *Amsterdam*, [20] and afterwards, signed books for the large turnout. The rains poured down hard tonight, but even though I had to drive a ways to Seattle, I knew I owed it to MAD (Martin Amis Discussion) to make it to the reading and report on the online message board about McEwan's appearance.

I parked near Pioneer Square, a notorious, sketchy area in downtown Seattle, and, like a naive neophyte in my Donna Karen mini-power suit, I walked through the tree-shaded square where transients and homeless hung out. A scruffy bearded man asked me for "change," but I was too nervous to get into my purse so I quickly tapped-danced away on my 4-inch heels across the square's redbrick ground to the bookstore on the corner.

I entered the door and went downstairs where Ian McEwan was scheduled to read in twenty minutes. The room was already filled with Seattle's literati, McEwan fans, and TV cameramen from Vancouver

---

20 Ian McEwan. *Amsterdam*. New York: Nan A. Talese/Doubleday; Dec. 1, 1998

BC for Bravo TV and the CBC (Canada). While talking with the house manager standing next to a velvet roped-off section, suddenly, out of nowhere, Ian McEwan walked by. I'm stunned, but there he was, crossing the bookstore basement floor, literally two feet in front of me.

Straight away I opened the portfolio I had under my arm and went up to Ian to show him a photo page from British *GQ* magazine of himself and Martin Amis at a party in a posh London men's club. He looked at the photo and wanted to know where it was taken. I queried, "Don't you remember?" He looked again, and then I ventured, "It may have been at The Groucho Club in London." Ian eyed it more closely and said, "Oh, it was at London's Polish Club where Martin had his opening party for *Money*." Not to be contrary, I nodded politely, but the caption clearly said it was taken at a press party for *London Fields*. I asked him if Martin and Julian (Barnes) were speaking again, and he looked quite seriously at me, shaking his head side to side, and replied a two-syllable "No-o."

Then I asked if he had spoken to Martin, and Ian immediately shot back, "Oh yes! He's my good friend."

I told him I was flying to Oxford next week to see Martin, and Ian informed me as he started up the stairs, "Martin is coming here!"

I quickly retorted, "I know, I meant Oxford, Mississippi, in the United States, where he's starting an American book tour."

"Oh-h yes," he said, and continued up the stairs.

Ian joined a camera crew that filmed him being interviewed. About fifteen minutes later, he passed by me again on his way to the auditorium.

I asked him, "Do you ever read MAD? It's the Martin Amis Discussion message board."

He looked at me inquisitively, so I explained.

"On the Internet. It's a website where we talk about Martin and his books, it was created by Professor James Diedrick. He wrote *Understanding Martin Amis*."

Walking on, Ian shot back: "Oh! I will have to tease him about it."

Minutes later I went back downstairs to the Elliott Bay Bookstore reading room, an auditorium filled with rows of wooden chairs surrounding a low platform for the author, and found a chair diagonal to the podium, second row back.

The house MC introduced Mr. McEwan who was greeted with a hearty applause by more than a hundred people in the audience. McEwan is slightly built, upper-class-slim, about five feet nine; a youngish fifty-one, wearing round, metal trimmed glasses and sporting a stylish haircut. I found him attractive in a British sort of way.

McEwan began reading the first chapter of *Amsterdam* as we all sat respectfully entertained by his Oxfordian, modulated voice. He read from his novel for almost an hour. Like most authors, Ian is not a trained actor, but his punched, dramatic reading showed he wanted to please his audience, and he did.

One memorable sentence described a character, the newspaperman Vernon: "He'd send the paper to the grave in perfect syntax." The room filled with laughter while I thought only of with my own faulty grammar on the MAD message board.

When the reading opened up for Q and A, the host asked us to be brief since this was the author's last stop before returning to London the next day, and as expected, he was fatigued from a long American book tour.

Suddenly, out of the nowhere, a strident voice rang out sharply, "WHAT IS THE POINT?"

McEwan heard the disheveled, gray haired woman who had shouted the question, and was taken-back, as we all were, and replied, "My book? …To entertain, I guess." The old woman looked mentally deranged and blurted out: "It certainly didn't deserve the Booker!"

The room sat appalled at her sudden rude outburst, and the author was clearly shaken. Who wouldn't be? (A woman in the signing line later commented to me she saw his face blush.) A din of disapproval, shudders, and excited whispers hovered over the room.

I turned around in my seat toward the harridan and heard myself say, "If you didn't like it, then why don't you go home?" She must've heard me, but did not reply.

It was the distinct, conspicuous moment of the evening but Mr. McEwan quickly composed himself and proceeded to ask for more questions from the audience. The abject interjection from the old crone hovered over the room, and none of us, including Ian, completely recovered from it. He explained the title, *Amsterdam,* to man who asked about it. I elaborated in a post on MAD after I read the novel. It has to do with legalized euthanasia in the progressive country. (What exactly *is* illegal in the ultra-permissive country?)

Waiting for McEwan to sign my copy of *Amsterdam,* a CBC director from Vancouver BC interviewed me on camera, along with others in the long line. He told us the production would be seen on the Bravo TV channel next month.

At Ian's signing desk, I felt compelled to remark, "Your audience enjoyed your reading very much, Ian. I am sorry for the intrusion from that horrible woman. I'm sure you have the mentally ill and crazies in England, too."

Ian replied, "Oh yes. I wrote a whole book about them."

The lady I had met in line kindly drove me to my parked car. As we turned the corner, Ian McEwan came out of the bookstore between two men, crossing the avenue. Impulsively, I rolled down the car window and yelled out, "Seattle loves you, Ian!"

His refined and serious face broke into a huge smile and he waved at me.

Twenty-Four

Martin Amis in Oxford, Mississippi

Martin Amis was coming to Oxford. Except this time, it was Oxford, Mississippi—not the famous Oxford University in England, but the University of Mississippi, "Ole Miss"—the indomitable icon of the Old South. Martin was scheduled to read from his new collection, *Heavy Water and Other Stories,* at the Oxford Square Bookstore across from the town square that still hung the South's Civil War Confederate flag waving.

I had left California to return to the Pacific Northwest to take care of my mother who insisted on living in her home of forty years. Mom had always said, "Promise me you won't ever put me in a nursing home!" and I ensured her she would live out her days in her own home.

The first thing I did after the moving truck brought my stuff from L.A. was to buy a computer. I chose an Apple Macintosh—a Mac—because it was advertised "User Friendly." I immediately signed up for America Online like everyone else did after AOL made its seminal debut on the Internet in the early nineties. Soon after, someone on my buddy list told me about an online message board called Martin Amis Discussion—or MAD—as members referred to the forum about their favorite modern author. I fit right in with the other misfits and weirdoes who were online during all hours of the night.

Julia Clinch

The new experience of chatting with people online that shared my interests—whom I'd never met and probably never would—was my main social activity since I'd moved back to my hometown. After being gone for twenty years I'd lost contact with people I'd known growing up and gone to school with. Old schoolmates had moved away or had busy careers and families of their own, so I didn't have a lot in common with them. As Frederick Exley, Jr., expressly wrote in his brilliant memoir, *A Fan's Notes*:

> *I had been unable to engage my hometown with any degree of openness. What friends I had had were married, raising families, and had locked themselves, ever so tightly, behind their neat-trimmed lawns and white clapboard houses, their children cute, their wives sexless and anxious, my friends plotting their next moves to achieve the local country club, never asking themselves what, if they achieve that—the town's most venerable institution—could possibly be left for them.* [21]

In addition to the town astronomy club—a grunge-clad group of sky watchers who all owned their own telescopes, I joined the local Great Books Discussion group. For the most part I went online for virtual social contact. I signed up for an AOL book club, which eventually led to being recruited to be its host every Friday night for the next ten years.

The online group was called the After Hours Book Club and consisted of night owls like me from all over the country (Chicago, New York, San Francisco, and small towns in Ohio, Missouri, the San Fernando Valley in Los Angeles and the Bay Area of northern California). In an online chat room, we discussed books we had chosen to read for that month.

One member of the After Hours Book Club was Vicki, a high school science teacher in Louisiana with whom I developed a long, online friendship. When I took a trip to New Orleans I visited Vicki and her husband who lived in St. Amant near Baton Rouge. It was right after Hurricane Katrina had hit the Louisiana and Mississippi coasts and continued

---

21   Frederick Exley, Jr., *A Fan's Notes: A Fictional Memoir*, New York: Harper & Row; 1968.

reconstruction and cleanup of the devastation from the flooding when the levies broke. Spending my holiday and money in New Orleans was my way to donate to the restoration of the hurricane-damaged city.

We planned for Vicki's husband, Delmar, to pick me up in the lobby of my New Orleans hotel in the French Quarter and then drive to his motorboat he moored in a backwater bayou south of Baton Rouge. Driving from New Orleans to his boat, I was comfortable with Delmar whom I'd just met that morning, but apprehensive to get into a small boat and stream along the swampy bayous; but there was no turning back. Delmar was eager to show me the alligators, herons, and wildlife of his south Louisiana parish. A dirt road took us to a wooded area where we arrived at the boating dock.

Delmar parked the car and we got into his small fishing boat. He steered the outboard engine as we explored the bifurcated, mossy waterways, which eventually flowed into the Gulf of Mexico. It was a new experience for me to ride the Louisiana backwaters and watch the indigenous wildlife, flora and fauna, and alligators. Seeing a large alligator near the shore, sitting next to a stranger in a boat flush with floating lily pads was unforgettable.

After spending several hours in the boat in the bayou sun, soaking up its reflected violet rays from the murky waters, my already tan skin turned a darker golden brown. In the afternoon Delmar drove me back to my hotel in New Orleans where I changed into a sundress and walked to Lafayette Square in the French Quarter to visit the historical New Orleans museums, and antebellum buildings.

As I handed my ticket to an African-American man at Lafayette Square museum door, he commented, "I like your skin." He caught me off guard to the compliment, but I thanked him.

He then advised, "If you were a little darker, you could apply for FEMA."

FEMA is the Federal Emergency Management Agency, an agency of the U.S. Homeland Security that was handing out $2,000 or more in cash or money orders—in addition to supplies and services—to victims of Hurricane Katrina; basically, to anybody who stood in the queue.

Vicki and Delmar visited me in my two-bedroom suite in the French Quarter and we walked to famous Antoine's restaurant, where we enjoyed a delicious French dinner. We then walked down the Quarter's lively Bourbon Street and heard some good jazz. In the morning Delmar drove us back to St. Amant and to the Barton Rouge airport where I flew back to Seattle. I had a wonderful time.

Once back home, I resumed taking care of mother and the dogs. Oprah Winfrey had launched her book club on AOL, so I became an Oprah Book Host. Oprah book hosts had to take more online training courses for Terms of Service: no harassment, no profanity, no marketing, no chain mail, no threats to the U.S. president, etc. I liked meeting readers as a volunteer for the book club every Friday night—all for the love of reading.

After I'd been hosting Oprah's Online Book Club for a year, a conference for the hosts was going to be held in Nashville, Tennessee. All Oprah's hosts were invited to attend a three-day weekend of festivities and social activities in the country-music capital of the world.

As fate would have it, the MAD board announced that Martin Amis would be at "Ole Miss," the University of Mississippi during the same week of Oprah's conference in Nashville. This was a staggering coincidence I couldn't pass up! Martin was going to give a reading at the Oxford Square Bookstore in Oxford, Mississippi, the same week as Oprah's Book Club conference in Nashville. (If I believed in psychic phenomena, I'd say this was a spot on.)

I looked at a map of Tennessee and Mississippi and saw that Nashville was about a hundred miles up from Oxford, Mississippi—not far for a nice, leisurely ride on the Mississippi State highway—not far, indeed.

In the meantime I'd begun to chat online on the MAD message board with both Travis, a young man who lived in Georgia, and Robert, a graduate student in English literature at the university in Hattiesburg, Mississippi. Robert had posted on a subject thread, "Martin in Oxford, Miss" that he was going to drive through Jackson, the capital of Mississippi, on his way to attend Martin's reading; he also planned to visit William Faulkner's house, Rowan Oak, located a few miles outside of Oxford, Ms., where the Nobel Prize winner wrote his literary masterpieces. I asked Robert if I could join him in Jackson, and would gladly pay for gas on the road trip to Oxford. Robert replied it was fine with him to meet in Jackson, and drive up to Ole Miss together. I made reservations at the downtown Ramada Inn in Jackson, and booked a ticket to Jackson, Mississippi, with a return flight from Nashville, Tennessee, where I planned to attend the Oprah Book Club conference the weekend after Martin's reading in Oxford. Now I knew someone in the Deep South—I had a MAD friend in Mississippi.

Travis (in Georgia) and I got into friendly debate on MAD about horses that progressed into a hilarious argument. We started discussing a chapter we'd both read in Tom Wolfe's novel, *A Man in Full* (1998; Farrar, Straus & Giroux.) We disagreed on how horses mated. After alternating posts disputing who knew more about the reproduction act of horses, Travis told me he would meet me at the Oxford Square Bookstore with irrefutable proof that he was correct how baby horses were made, and that I didn't know what I was talking about.

"How will I recognize you?" I asked Travis.

"I'll be the only one in the bookstore wearing a horse costume."

• • •

My trip to the Deep South was planned for a week of new experience and adventure. I'd always wanted to visit the American Deep South and now I had an opportunity to attend two events in the south that I couldn't have dreamed to take place the same week.

Mother's dementia was progressing, although she could function fairly well in her own home. Whenever I could get away for a respite, I'd pay a neighbor or cousin to take care of Mom and our pets during a short absence. It was not always easy to find someone who would come over every day whom I felt was trustworthy and reliable.

Meanwhile, I had bought Mom an African Gray parrot for Mother's Day to keep her company. We named him Bo bin Laden because he was a "tear-o-rist"– tearing up whatever he could get his beak and talons on. Bo Laden spoke in clear sentences, continuously asking Mom questions like, "What's your problem?" She engaged conversations with Bo, and we all enjoyed him as one of the family. Once, after I came home from a short excursion, I was dusting near the parrot cage when Bo screamed, "You little shit!" I did a one-eighty toward the parrot, knowing I had not taught him to say that expletive and immediately telephoned his last caretaker, Kathleen. She admitted she had yelled that at him, and told me, "Your possessed parrot tried to bite me!"

The day of my departure for Oxford, Mississippi, finally arrived and I took the airport shuttle to SeaTac—Seattle-Tacoma Airport. After several hours flying southeast—with a short layover in Montgomery, Alabama— the 707 landed in Jackson, Mississippi airport. It was already dark when I took a cab to the downtown Jackson Ramada Inn and checked in. After depositing my suitcase in my hotel room, I took off my clothes and shoes, got on top of the bed and turned on the TV. Ironically, *Mississippi Burning*, a brutal film about race and civil rights in the Deep South, was showing.

I wasn't going to watch a movie about racial violence in past-segregated Mississippi—especially while I was *in* Mississippi—so I got dressed and left the room. I followed the sound of loud music coming from the cocktail lounge off the lobby. A five-piece band blasted from speakers on a small stage—two guitarists were belting out a Beach Boys song in the mostly empty barroom. Small tables were scattered around the room with a few beer-bellied geezers guzzling from the beer bottles, oblivious of the music blaring from the stage.

Hearing a Beach Boys song in Jackson, Mississippi, did not do it for me, so I immediately went up to the bartender.

"Excuse me, sir, but I didn't come all the way from the Pacific Coast to hear a Mississippi band play the Beach Boys!"

He grinned and told me to ask the band to play something else.

After they finished the song, I walked up to lead singer and nicely asked , "Could you please play some real Southern music? Anything country or rock and roll?"

The band obliged me with "Sweet Home Alabama." Finally, I felt like I was in the Deep South.

A burly, good ol' boy that was watching my actions came over and said, "I'd like you to meet someone," and took me to two big, middle-aged boys seated at a small table near the bar. I sat down and we exchanged salutations, "When you get here? Can I buy you a drink?"

The larger man told me his name was 'Bubba' (imagine that). After we talked a while, Bubba struck me as the man in charge around this neck of the woods, having lived here all his life, as had his bloodline for generations gone back.

Hearing my Northern accent, the big, salt-and-pepper-whisker Bubba reckoned I was a "Yankee from the Union," for which he'd held a standing resentment since the Civil War—even though it had ended long before he was born.

Taking a swig from his glass of whiskey, Bubba promptly informed me, "We have three kinds of people 'round here—city folks, country folks, and niggers."

I sensed Bubba was goading me—a nigra' lovin' Yankee—to react to his blatant racism; but instead of taking the bait, I replied, "Okay," in a so-what-tone.

I could tell Bubba was taken back by my indifference, but respected my handling his contentious polemic with nonchalance. As labeled a "Yankee-woman's libber," I wasn't going to start a civil rights protest in a Mississippi bar with a big redneck named Bubba. Instead, I deferred to Bubba's right to hold court as he saw fit in his own domain and express his Jim Crow views, although I did not share them. Bubba continued talking politics, which led to his opinion about Lyndon B. Johnson: "Why do you like LBJ?" he demanded to know, as if to say, "How could you—after what that traitor did to the South?"

Again I didn't want to start a barroom fight about the civil rights laws that LBJ expedited through Congress, so I said, "Before Lyndon Johnson was president, he was a high school teacher like me, and we want American kids to have an opportunity for a good education. And if you don't agree with that, let's take this outside!"

Bubba gave me a big, southern hospitality smile, and exclaimed, "I like you!"

When it was time to leave, I told Bubba it was nice talking with him, but I was going to go to Oxford in the morning, and called it a night. A true gentleman, Mr. Bubba paid for my drink and insisted on walking me through the hotel lobby down the hall to my room. Standing in front of the door, Bubba kissed my hand and said, "A real pleasure meeting you, Ma'am. Have a good trip in the morning." A true diamond-in-the-rough, Bubba was a bona-fide Southern man.

• • •

The next morning Robert was waiting for me in the hotel lobby at 10 a.m. as we agreed. After checking out of the hotel, we started the long drive up to Oxford, Mississippi, with plans to stop at Rowan Oak, the home of William Faulkner, before driving a few more miles to Ole Miss to attend Martin Amis reading that evening at Oxford Square Bookstore.

As Robert drove north up the modern Mississippi highway, I looked out the window to see many miles of immaculate farmland, pristine fields, and small towns on the rural landscape.

"Everything looks so pleasant and maintained. I'm surprised, because Mississippi is usually portrayed as being backwater and the poorest state in the union."

"That's because the State sued the tobacco companies for the responsibility of all the lung cancer patients in Mississippi and putting the burden of health-care costs on the taxpayers."

"Could they really do that and win their case?"

"Not only did they prove it, but the State won billions of dollars from the tobacco industry and put it back into the infrastructure of Mississippi. That's what you're seeing now."

"I imagine the school system is much better, being able to improve the schools and pay teachers more; the whole state must be on a par or better than other states now."

"You got that right."

After a few more hours on the brand-new Mississippi highway, we saw a sign that read "Oxford – 30 Miles." Farther on, we saw another sign: "William Faulkner House—Next Left." Robert exited the Interstate to a two-lane road that displayed a wooden post pointed to the Nobel Prize author's home. We turned onto a dirt road, and through tall oak trees, I saw Rowan Oak, William Faulkner's pre-Civil War home, he had bought in 1930.

We parked on the side of the dirt road. The two-story, simple Greek-revival house resembled most ante-bellum Southern homes. Faulkner's 19th century country home was dignified, but not stately, as I had imagined it. The horse carriage house off to the side was surrounded by oak shade trees and uncultivated land. We walked to the covered veranda that welcomed visitors and paid the lady seated on the porch the five-dollar donation, and entered the old house.

The door opened into a central hallway extending to the opposite end of the house. (Many old Southern homes are called "shotgun houses" because you could shoot off a rifle from the front door straight through to the backdoor without hitting a wall.) The living room, parlor, dining room, kitchen, and writing den were situated off the long hallway. The interior of the house was well preserved with the original, furnished rooms roped off from entrance.

I peered into the first room on the right, which appeared to be a parlor with Queen Anne chairs and a small, brick fireplace. I glanced inside to the far-right corner and saw a Japanese geisha doll in a rectangular glass case on a little table. World War II soldiers returning from Japan often brought back these geisha dolls as souvenirs for their mothers, wives, and daughters.

The dining room was on the other side of the hallway, the table set with fine English china and silverware. As we proceeded down the hall, a small, nicely dressed Japanese couple entered the museum house speaking in their native language. I walked over and motioned for them to look inside the parlor where the Japanese statuette was on display. When the little couple saw the encased geisha doll, their faces lit up in a wave of patriotism and they muffled sounds of national pride.

Robert and I continued the tour of the home that led to the last room off the hallway the guide said was Faulkner's writing room. The room was austere with only a wooden desk and the author's original Underwood typewriter on which he punched out his masterpieces. My favorite Faulkner novel is *The Sound and the Fury*; to me, he conveyed human nature as well as his namesake, William Shakespeare. Faulkner had worn out a pair of men's weathered, lace-up shoes that were placed next to a wall. A small, picture calendar hung on the faded wallpaper from a bygone year in the author's life. The privilege of being in William Faulkner's home was an honor and highlight in my life.

Oxford, Mississippi

Robert and I continued on the road to Oxford and checked into a hotel near the Ole Miss. We arrived a few hours before Martin's reading at the Square Bookstore, so I had time to shower and change into a clean blouse and long skirt before walking around Oxford's quaint downtown area. Like most old Southern towns and those along the Mississippi River, Oxford was a provincial town that radiated out from a central town square. The shops, streets, and public buildings had been through decades, many built before the Civil War, but well maintained by the city and University of Oxford. The students at Ole Miss and town inhabitants were friendly and hospitable to an out-of-towner, a Yankee, like myself, greeting "Good day" as they passed.

When it was almost time for the honored speaker to read, I walked to the Square Bookstore and saw Martin coming down the sidewalk with a slim, young woman wearing designer black slacks and a knit pullover. I assumed she was the assigned handler from his New York publisher since she certainly didn't blend with the denizens or students in town. I stood by the bookstore and waited for Martin to approach. His face was palpably startled when he saw me standing in front of him—unrelated to any context he had known me in. It took him a few seconds to recognize the unexpected apparition before him.

"Hi, Martin," I greeted, knowing he was set aback.

Hearing my voice, Martin looked pleasantly surprised, and immediately walked up and kissed my cheek. "What are you doing here?" he asked curiously in this new backdrop.

"I flew to see you in Oxford," I said, emphasizing the double entendre of its namesake city. "Plus, I've always wanted to visit the Deep South."

We exchanged "How are you's?" before the handler tapped his shoulder and pointed to the door. Martin excused himself and went inside for his reading. I followed him into the bookstore, found a seat in the front row, and sat down in one of the folding, wooden chairs that had been set up in many rows. I turned around to see the bookstore was filling up rapidly as people were looking for seats when I espied Robert sitting in the back row. In the next few minutes the bookstore was standing room only with Martin's fans that had come to see him in person.

After a glowing introduction, Martin walked to the podium in front of the room now crowded to the maximum and began reading from his latest collection, *Heavy Water and Other Stories,* in his melodic, British voice. In no time he had the entire Oxford bookstore in his hand—as he had captivated me many years before in his London flat. Martin read "A Janitor on Mars," a short story, and then took questions from the audience.

When Martin returned to sit in the first row across from me, a local banjo band played Cajun songs for the evening's entertainment: one man strummed a washboard as he hummed on a held-up harmonica while the other musicians played banjo and fiddle. I looked over to see Martin's response to this backwoods concert and his face showed he was enjoying the down-home music. Maybe Martin's countenance was affected out of courtesy for the musicians and audience, but he appeared to truly like the Cajun concert his hosts had chosen for him.

After Martin signed books for the long queue that had stretched around the room, I asked if Robert and I could have a drink with him. To my chagrin, he said a private party had been planned for him after the reading, which he was on the way to.

"Holy Moses, Martin, I flew all the way from Seattle to see you!" This was half true.

Martin was taken back at my outburst. Realizing I overreacted, I calmed down and said, "Good to see you, Martin," and left to find Robert.

As the crowd slowly dispersed, I saw Robert in the back of the bookstore, pleased to have gotten several of Martin's books signed that he had brought with him. When I told him Martin had left for a party at a restaurant in town, we were both determined to find it. After peering inside the bar room of the rowdy restaurant next door and not seeing Martin or a party, we got into Robert's car and drove around Oxford's small downtown. I went in and out of a few restaurants and bars looking for Martin while Robert waited in the car. Disappointed we were unable to find Martin or the party, we returned to the restaurant next door to the bookstore and went in.

This time I walked up to the bartender and asked if he knew about a party for Martin Amis around town. The manager heard me and pointed to the staircase to the second floor, and said, "Everyone's upstairs."

Relieved we had finally found the place (where we had started out), Robert and I climbed the dark stairwell to find a lively, upstairs room with a long bar and small tables filled with partying customers on their second or third drinks. A corner area was partitioned off on the side of the room and we could see Martin through sheer curtains seated at a round table, surrounded by his hosts, colleagues, and ever-present, codependent handler. Martin was holding the largest, stemmed goblet I'd ever seen, filled with vodka, perhaps a breath of vermouth, and green olive.

Robert and I found an empty table where we could view Martin more clearly. Robert sat in the chair while I sat on the wooden bench affixed to the paneled wall.

Now that we had found Martin we relaxed and ordered drinks so we could watch him through the curtained partition; technically, we were drinking with Martin. Robert tried to discern if he could recognize any of the guests at Martin's table.

Then, suddenly out-of-nowhere in the darkened lounge, Martin appeared instantaneously at our table, slid onto the bench next to me and asked straight out, "What did you mean on my message machine when you said, "This is Mrs. Julian Barnes?'" He was still holding the enormous martini glass.

Surprised at the sudden intrusion, I was speechless. Here at my side was Martin, tactically flanking my right hip, demanding forthright an explanation about the message I had left on his answering machine over a year ago when I called him from Myra's flat (again—one block parallel to his writing flat in Notting Hill).

I did not know what to reply in this explosive confrontation. However, I did *not* say I was Mrs. Julian Barnes in the message, but that I knew how *Julian Barnes felt* (about Martin's betrayal). Martin had mistakenly heard, "Mrs." Julian Barnes on the voice mail. Was this misunderstanding Freudian? After all, he had ditched his longtime literary agent for the slick New Yorker.

Martin left the table without getting an answer, leaving Robert and me stunned, but also enthralled by the dramatic scene we had just witnessed. No doubt Martin had had a couple of those gigantic martinis and may not remember his dramatic appearance at our table, but it happened, as Robert was my witness.

Still trying to process the encounter, Robert and I finished our drinks and called it a night. We drove to our Oxford hotel and retired to our respective rooms, exhausted from the day's exuberant experience. I paid for Robert's room since he had driven me to Oxford and now offered to drive me to Nashville to attend Oprah's Book Club conference. In the morning I filled the car's gas tank, and we headed north up the smooth Mississippi interstate to Tennessee.

• • •

"Doesn't Texas sometimes seem to resemble a country
like Saudi Arabia, with its great heat, its oil wealth, its
brimming houses of worship, and its weekly executions?"

— MARTIN AMIS

To answer your cheeky analogy: No, Mart, inalienable rights are guaranteed in Texas by the Ten Amendments to the U.S. Constitution: among which are freedom of speech, the right to bear arms, and freedom of the press. These freedoms do not exist in Saudi Arabia. If you wrote about politics there–as you often do here–or criticized the Saudi king or royal family, you would be fatwa'd like Salman Rushdie. Allah forbid, you blasphemed the state religion or its prophet the way you disparage religion in America. A public display that would involve a sharp sword would submit you to Shari'ah law. Texas has its own brand of religious dogma, but it is not written in blood, nor does it have "religious police" on the streets. Where would you live, Mart, to have the freedom to write, to criticize, and kvetch? Love, Jules

Twenty-Five

An Evening with Martin Amis and Christopher Hitchens at UCLA

My friendship with the Hitch has always
been perfectly cloudless.
It is a love whose month is ever May.

— Martin Amis, *The Independent* 2007

After twenty years of living in L.A., I had moved on, or should I say life had moved me on. I had returned to my hometown in Washington to take care of my mother whose health was slowly diminishing. After nine years of being mother's only caretaker, she passed away. Losing your mother is a major milestone in one's life, no matter how much you prepare for it—or feel about them. Life isn't the same without your mother in it. Afterwards I continued to live in the house that mother had treasured and loved for more than forty years.

In the meantime, I'd been dating Ron, a forty-nine-year-old man who was also taking care of his elderly parents. I needed a companion while I took care of mother, especially during times of emotional cruelty from the faraway, guilt-ridden 'sinisister,' e.g., hateful threats, closing mom's bank accounts, false reports to authorities, etc. After several months of

Ron asking me to dinner, I accepted his invitation. We dated and got along, mostly because I wasn't in love with him, but regarded Ron as a friend. We took road trips to Reno and around Washington State. After Ron moved his parents into an assisted-living facility, we traveled out of the country: Cabo San Lucas, Mexico; London, England; and all over Germany. When we returned from Europe, Ron continued to live in his parents' home while I stayed with my pets in the house that mother had bequeathed to me.

Ron knew I had interviewed Martin Amis in London, but not much more. When Martin was coming to Seattle on a book tour for his new novel, *Yellow Dog*,[22] ꟺI said I was going to the Elliott Bay Bookstore to see him. Ron immediately got jealous and told me I couldn't go. He was being unreasonable. I had made up my mind to attend the reading, and he was welcome to go with me.

On the evening of Martin's arrival, we drove to Seattle (Ron had decided to come along—to keep an eye on me). By the time the reading and audience Q and A were over, Ron no longer thought Martin was a threat. He told me Martin had "hobbled to the book signing table." In fact, Ron realized he had overreacted and that I could not possibly be attracted to this writer so he bought a copy of *Yellow Dog*, and was first in line to have Martin sign it; he did, not knowing *who* Julie was: "To Julie, Regards, Martin Amis."

Ron had proposed more than twice and had given me a diamond ring, but I told him I didn't want to get married again. I considered him as a friend, not as a potential husband. After the rejection, Ron began to make frequent, mysterious disappearances, although I did not question his whereabouts. By now, like a dead owl, I didn't give a hoot.

In spring 2003, I read that Martin and Christopher Hitchens were going to talk on stage at my alma mater, UCLA, on April 20. The event was advertised as "An Evening with Martin Amis and Christopher

---

22 Martin Amis. *Yellow Dog*. New York: Miramax Books, (2003)
ꟺ "And a fine race (French) it is! - the finest in the world, and anyone who says different is a yellow dog."

Hitchens at UCLA." I immediately bought a ticket online for this once-in-a-lifetime event.

When I told Ron I was going, he put his foot down: "No, you're not!"

I looked at him, "Are you kidding me?" He acted as if he could tell me when, where, and what I could do, while he went off to unknown places all day. He was definitely getting on my nerves.

A week before the UCLA event, Ron picked a fight about my computer he was sharing at my house and stormed out. I couldn't understand why he was acting like a child—using such an insignificant reason to leave. All I knew was that Ron was acting strangely. Because of his vehement protest, I had actually considered not going to see Martin and Hitchens, but now Ron's puerile behavior made me wonder why I listened to his influence? While he was gone I booked a round-trip flight to Los Angeles to see Martin and Hitchens at UCLA. When Ron returned later that night, I told him I was going and he flipped out. I calmly informed him I had no idea where he had gone when he flew out the door, so he was in no position to tell me where I could not go. I was flying to L.A., end of story.

Months later, I found out that Ron was a compulsive gambler. He had been frequenting a gaming casino and had suffered huge gambling losses. Using the power of attorney he had for his parents, he had "borrowed" (his word) both his mother's monthly Social Security and his father's Boeing pension to finance his gambling addiction. I informed him that in order to borrow money, you had to first ask permission from the lender; otherwise, it was embezzlement or theft.

On the afternoon of the big event, my plane landed at LAX and I took a cab to the Beverly Hills Ramada Inn, where I had reserved a room. After showering and reapplying my makeup, I put on a little black dress and my new *peau de soie* pumps. The hotel concierge called a taxi to take me to UCLA, a short distance away in Westwood. On the way in the cab, my iPhone rang. Answering, I could hear boisterous male voices carousing in the background, but couldn't make out exactly what the commotion was. It sounded like a drunken orgy. The caller ID showed Ron's cell number; apparently, it had been a pocket call. I later learned Ron was at his favorite casino, gambling with his cronies, whom he would eventually join at Gamblers Anonymous—not as jubilantly—but as defeated losers.

When the taxi stopped in front of the UCLA campus in Westwood Village, I was surprised to see how much construction had been built since I had graduated decades before. Several high-rise buildings had been erected on campus since I had left my alma mater. Many new buildings surrounded the high Student Union of my college years. (I had gone up in its elevator with once-called, basketball legend, Lou Alcindor. I remember looking at his belt buckle due to our different heights). The West entrance of the campus where I had walked from my off-campus apartment was barely recognizable.

"An Evening with Martin Amis and Christopher Hitchens" was to be held in Royce Hall, where, in my undergraduate years, I had attended lectures and classes in the Lombardi-Romanesque edifice. Even after thirty years, I knew exactly where Royce Hall was located and headed uphill toward the iconic landmark. Walking up the campus path, I passed dozens of students' signs: announcements of organized protests, political demonstrations, and campus fraternity and sorority functions. Suddenly, on the left, the spectacular, old-world architecture of Royce Hall stood high in the foreground and I followed the walkway to the magnificent site.

Walking into the arched-ceiling vestibule, I handed my ticket to a student standing by one of the Renaissance double doors. Déjà vu emerged as I entered the long lobby with its wax-polished, hardwood floors and paneled walls. The pervasive aroma pervaded my being, flooding my mind and senses with bygone time—my own *Remembrance of Things Past*—reminiscent of the memories of Marcel Proust. Overwhelmed by sensuous nostalgia of long past days inside these walls, a gravitation propelled me to the refreshment bar where I ordered a glass of champagne.

Looking back I probably shouldn't have drunk alcohol in my intensely anticipated mood, but I did. Sipping bubbly from a plastic, stemmed flute, I watched hordes of well-heeled people, as well as scruffy stragglers who looked like the grandchildren of sixties flower children or Jerry Garcia's illegitimate progeny walk into the wide rectangular lobby of Royce Hall. The crowd looked eager to spend an evening with Martin and "The Hitch." After I swigged down the champagne, I entered the auditorium, walked down to the middle fourth row and took my seat.

Eagerly waiting for the event to begin, the din of auditorium voices began to lull. I turned around and saw a conspicuous, middle-age couple being rush-ushered down the side aisle, and immediately recognized—along with everyone else—Hollywood power couple: actor Warren Beatty and his wife, Annette Bening, as they quickly took their seats.

Minutes after the spectacle of the Beatty-Bening fashionably-late entrance, the lights in Royce Hall dimmed, and the stage, heavy, velvet curtains slowly parted, revealing Martin Amis and Christopher Hitchens sitting in red leather Queen Anne chairs, aside two small tables. The authors each held a Styrofoam cup.

Martin and Christopher promptly began to engage the audience in entertaining stories about their long friendship, telling personal anecdotes and disputations they had on various topics that they shared over the past several decades. They discussed each other's political positions and disagreements as they drank from the white cups throughout the dialogue.

Hitchens defended his case for the war in Iraq, a topic that was currently being debated in the mainstream media: Should the United States return to Iraq after the first Desert Storm war to overthrow its dictator, Saddam Hussein? Advocates believed there was the imminent threat of weapons of mass destruction Saddam might deploy against America and Israel. The dictator had been in power for twenty-five years, and had shown brutality to his own people when he gassed thousands of Kurds in their villages, including innocent women and children. Hitchens talked about his Kurdish friends and was in favor of proactive aggressive to topple Iraq's dictator. Martin did not agree with a preemptive act of war from the Bush administration, convinced that the rumors of WMDs were mere saber rattling in spite of the ominous circumstances. Hitchens rebutted this with reports Saddam would not allow the United Nations inspectors to examine his atomic arsenals that official UN regulations had stipulated.

Changing the subject, Martin talked about a road trip that he and Hitchens had taken to visit Saul Bellow and his fourth wife in his home in Vermont. Martin had besieged Hitchens not to go off on a political screed when they got to Bellow's home. (Hitchens political position was far left at the time—opposite of Bellow's.) Hitchens assured Martin he would be respectful to his host and not instigate a contentious dispute with Saul. Of course, that's exactly what he did after they arrived and sat down to drink cocktails in the Bellow living room.[23]

By now, Martin had the audience in tow, and announced:

"2003 has been The Year of the Pirate. Not only has Johnny Depp made *Pirates of the Caribbean,* but Paul McCartney has married a woman with one leg." The auditorium roared.

Favorite debates of the gruesome twosome included "Who was the more evil dictator of the twentieth century: Hitler or Stalin?" Martin opted for Stalin, while Hitchens elected Hitler. Martin had written *Koba the Dread: Laughter and the Twenty Million,* [24] an account of Stalin's iron-handed reign over the USSR. During Stalin's long dictatorship (Stalin means "steel" in Russian), twenty-million farmers in the Ukraine starved to death after the state expropriated grain and livestock from their farms to feed the huge, populated Soviet nation for Stalin's "five-year plan" goal of Communism. Farmers and their families were left to starve after

---

23 "Amis wrote about Hitchens and Bellow in *Experience: A Memoir* (2000). Hitchens described it in *Hitch-22.* Bellow's perspective is in *Saul Bellow: Letters,* in a letter to Cynthia Ozick, August 29, 1989: "Amis had invited Hitchens, his best friend, to join him for dinner at Bellow's Vermont home. On the ride there, Amis warned Hitchens that he 'wasn't to drag the conversation toward anything political, let alone left-wing, let alone anything to do with Israel.' But before dinner, Hitchens spotted something that would soon set him off:" – Rick Richman, "Bellow, Hitchens, and COMMENTARY." *Commentary Magazine,* Nov. 8, 2010. https://www.commentarymagazine.com/culture-civilization/literature/bellow-hitchens-and-commentary/

24 Martin Amis. *Koba the Dread: Laughter and the Twenty Million.* New York: Miramax, 2002.

eating what little livestock was left on their stripped land. Their children were not allowed out of the house for fear they would never be seen again. Documentation has shown the starving had turned to cannibalism, eating children and the dead. Eventually the USSR collapsed and fell in on itself. [25]

Hitchens rebutted Martin with his choice that Hitler was the more evil, maintaining Das Führer won the dubious title because—under his orders, The Holocaust eliminated ninety percent—an entire generation—of European Jews. The Final Solution was Hitler's systematic annihilation of Jews, rounding up and transporting them by trains to concentration and death camps by Nazi SS soldiers (*Schutzstaffel.*) Martin agreed it was especially heinous that Jews had to buy their own one-way train tickets to a final destination from which they would not return.

After an hour and a half of witty exchanges and anecdotes by the hosts, the question and answer segment was opened for the audience. A middle-aged man stood up and asked:

"What's in those cups you're drinking?"

Hitchens answered, "Jim Beam."

The man followed up with the most interesting question of the evening: "Why?"

A woman in the audience brought up a word game Martin and Christopher played, which Hitchens had written about in his *Vanity Fair* column. The idea was to replace the word *heart* in the title of a popular song, book, or film with the word "dick."

She asked the writers, "Would you give us a few examples?"

Hitchens recognized the game and tossed out a meme of Tony Bennett's hit song, "I Left My Dick in San Francisco," followed by Carson McCullers' novel, "The Dick is a Lonely Hunter," and "Don't Go Breaking My Dick"—to the sheer delight of the audience.

---

25 Martin Amis. *House of Meetings.* London: Jonathan Cape Ltd., 2006. Set in Stalin's Soviet Gulag, the Siberian frozen penal colony where tens of thousands of Stalin's dissidents were sent who had not been summarily executed.

Martin volunteered his samples: "Your Cheatin' Dick," and "My Achy, Breaky Dick," to more peals of laughter.

When the event onstage concluded, a thunderous applause showered the writers. As people got up to leave, a dozen or so women, including myself, rushed down to the stage proscenium to bask in Hitchens' corona as he stood downstage. We took turns shooting questions in his piqued ears and ego. Hitchens, known to talk to anyone and everyone who wanted to engage his mental prowess, answered our questions, one after the other, enjoying us as much as we did him.

On the other side of the stage, Martin was un-surrounded—as it were, by no one. It reminded me of a scene in his novel, *The Information,* where the protagonist-author, Richard Tull, gave a reading to only four people seated in a small auditorium: a native American Indian (who soon left), a corpulent man, an African American ("as black as Adam") and a plus-size woman wearing a smock. Seeing Martin alone on the other side of the stage was a simulacrum of the scenario in the novel—compared to his rival, a prosaic writer who read to a sold-out audience in the large auditorium next door. Every time I read the passage I howl. It was poignant watching Martin standing alone while a covey of women fawned over Hitchens. Adding to the pathos, Martin saw me among those sucking up to Hitchens. Finally, Warren Beatty went up to Martin to shake his hand, and introduce himself. This was a huge relief to see Martin finally getting due attention—to wit, from a major movie star.

In the meantime, Hitchens said he had to find a restroom quickly and excused himself and left the stage. Most likely, he'd been drinking (alcohol) since early on that day. We followed The Hitch like ducklings to Mother Goose waddling up the backstage side stairs.

On the way I stopped by Martin who was still talking to Beatty on the left stage. When they saw me, I said hello to Warren and complemented Martin how entertaining he and Hitchens had been. Martin thanked me and went backstage, leaving me alone with Warren.

I asked him, "Do you remember me the time Jack Valenti and you visited the UCLA campus?"

(Urban legend has it that Warren has been with, allegedly, more than ten thousand women). He corrected me that we had met at USC. I reminded him I had attended UCLA where I had been a sophomore. Warren was positive which university it was, so I didn't argue with his prideful, but unreliable, memory (it had been his game to memorize phone numbers). Actually, we had met months before that at the Hamburger Hamlet where I had been working part-time and he had asked for my phone number.

Suddenly, his wife, Annette Bening, scurried down the aisle to Warren, interrupting us. Warren introduced me, "Annette, this is Julie," but Mrs. Beatty didn't even look my way, but continued talking to Warren as if I wasn't there. I didn't take her rudeness personally because it's a statistical probability that any woman over forty whom Warren introduced to his wife had had him before she did, including me.

Her disinterest implied 'leave us,' so I did, politely adding, "It was nice meeting you, Mrs. Beatty." She managed a glance as I walked up the staircase to see what Hitch was doing backstage with his fawning fans.

The same dozen women surrounded Hitchens; enraptured by the witty pearls he threw in their ears. Hitch was still looking for a restroom when I saw a sign on a wall marked MEN. I gestured to Hitch where it was, and he thanked me as he closed the door. While Hitch was in the restroom, I saw Mona Simpson from *The Atlantic* magazine talking to two UCLA academics with which she had organized the evening's event. Coincidentally, Mona Simpson (whose novel, *Anywhere but Here*, was made into a film starring Susan Sarandon and Natalie Portman) was the biological sister of Steve Jobs, the entrepreneur of Apple Computer. A couple in California had adopted Steve as a baby before Mona was born to their American mother and Syrian father after they married. Raised apart, both were gifted with extraordinary genes, and each became successful in their respective fields—especially Steve Jobs in Apple Computer. The young genius brought about a revolution in technological advances and communication across the world: e.g., MacBook, Pixar, the iPod, iPad and the iPhone.

When Hitchens came out, women were waiting, but before we could continue talking to him, Mona Simpson grabbed Hitch by the hand and led him to an exit door. Outside in the parking lot, a car with Martin and others in it was already waiting to drive them to an exclusive party at the W Hotel in Westwood Village, a few blocks from UCLA. I saw another car driving out of the lot and asked the man if I could have a ride to the W Hotel. He didn't know where it was, but I told him to please drop me off in Westwood. He said get in.

Minutes later, I thanked the gentleman for the ride and got out in Westwood Village, and began to look for the W hotel. I walked to Mario's Restaurant and asked a waiter for directions. He pointed to Highland Avenue—close to where the man had dropped me off. I walked back to Highland and immediately found the W hotel. The inside lobby was empty so I peered into the cocktail lounge to make out a handful of customers seated in the dark room.

By now I needed to powder my nose after the brisk walking. When I entered the ladies restroom, two, tall, young, black women were standing in front of the mirror. I began to apply lipstick, but distinctly felt the 'we were here first' looks, so I quickly left.

Frustrated that I still couldn't find the party for Martin and Hitchens, I asked the night clerk if there was a party in the hotel. He said it was on the terrace on the second floor and pointed me to the elevator. Relieved to finally find my goal, the elevator door opened to the mezzanine where a large terrace filled with partiers in full swing was visible behind a glass wall. I told the two women seated at the glass door with the guest list that I was an alumna of UCLA and knew the honored authors inside. Martin was talking with a man near the glass partition; when I waved hello, he waved back. One of the women kindly opened the door to the party. (Later, the same woman gave me her card and emailed me photographs taken of Martin, Christopher Hitchens, Michael York, and me.)

Martin at W party

Hitchens and me at W party

Visiting Martin Amis

• • •

The open-air terrace was buzzing with the chattering of East and West Coast literati. Celebrants and patrons of the arts engaged in cheery conversations, holding cocktails in plastic containers from the open bars. VIPs munched on hors d'oeuvres offered on trays by wandering, young caterers. I saw Hitchens—as usual, surrounded by a caravan of female groupies crowding around him like at UCLA—except these women were on the invitations-only guest list.

Walking past Hitchens' circle of feminine-fans, I went inside to the open bar in the adjoining room and asked for a cabernet. I overheard someone say Christopher Hitchens had gone straight to the bar when he arrived, ordered Jim Beam, and told the bartender, "You'll be seeing a lot of me."

After getting a drink, I went back outside to the open terrace and strolled among the well-heeled guests. Michael York was with an older, short, blond woman, while Warren Beatty was talking to a younger woman who had the distinct air of East Coast money. I nodded to Warren and continued to roam the crowded terrace until I saw a nest of women around Warren's wife, Annette Bening, listen to her swagger about her latest credits. Someone whispered that British actress, Tilda Swinton, was there.

Standing unnoticed among the women, I heard Annette tell the group about British journalist, Tina Brown (former editor of *Vanity Fair* and *The New Yorker*). Tina "had forged a partnership with Hearst Magazines and Hollywood producer Harvey Weinstein, the co-chairman of Miramax" ᵠ for backing to publish a glossy monthly magazine called *Talk*. Annette proudly told the women about her upcoming interview on Tina Brown's eponymous talk show on NBC (The show was cancelled after a few episodes, followed by the demise of *Talk* magazine soon afterwards.)

φ Alessandra Stanley. "Talk Ends and Spin Begins: Tina Brown Has No Regrets." New York Times http://www.nytimes.com/2002/01/20/us/talkand-spin-begins-tina-brown-has-no-regrets.html-ends-

I looked around for Hitchens when I saw his entourage across the terrace and walked over to join them. A frumpy, 'unpleasantly plump' woman in her thirties, wearing a floppy hat, was standing in the circle around Hitch.

Whispering behind in her ear, I asked, "Is this the Christopher Hitchens fan club?"

She mockingly replied, "No, it's Jews for Jesus!" I chuckled at her sarcastic remark, which instantly defused her snarky reply. She was speechless—surely one of the few times in her life.

'Floppy hat' is a typical spoiled Daddy's girl with an inflated ego, overbearing, and assertive. I often wonder how these women maintain an in your face self-righteousness in spite of being unattractive and an off-putting personality. Their doting father instilled early to her she was an American princess—entitled, as it were—throughout her privileged life. (Contrary to women whose fathers were disappointed we weren't born sons.)

Martin Amis and Michael York at UCLA party

Hitchens was holding steadfast his position favoring the Iraq War that had recently begun its shock and awe campaign. Hitchens had many Kurdish friends in northern Iraq whose families and children had been gassed by Saddam's planes, and had died agonizing deaths in the streets with other bodies rotting in the desert sun. In the past, Hitchens had been an unflagging liberal, but now he was at odds with the leftwing, antiwar faction in America and the UK. Hitchens had sympathies for the underdog, which manifested consistent with him supporting the Kurds who wanted Saddam Hussein taken down. Hitchens eagerly expressed his views on the Iraq war with anyone and whenever the subject came up.

My plastic flute empty, I walked back through the open partition to the bar for another cabernet. Standing at the bar, I spoke to a witty, middle-aged man who made me laugh. He was a few inches taller than me, with average looks, but I would've liked to have gotten to know him if I still lived in L.A.

Across the room I saw Martin seated on a divan, chatting with two attractive, young women sitting opposite him. I gestured with two closed fingers that I'd like a hand-rolled cigarette and he motioned for me to come over. I sat on the carpeted floor next to Martin while he lit a rollie and handed it to me while he continued talking to the young women. When I commented how shiny their hair was, they said they were models for Vidal Sassoon, the famous, hair stylist mogul. More small talk ensued until the hair models said they had to leave.

Martin lit me another cigarette, and suggested, "Let's go find Hitch."

Hitchens was on the terrace, this time with an amphitheater of mixed admirers hanging intently on his every word. Holding his perennial Styrofoam cup, Hitchens expounded even more vehemently why the Iraq War was necessary; by now his polemic was flavored with piss and vinegar. Hitch was determined to take on anyone who dared to challenge him.

Two bearded men in their thirties, looking like typical antiwar protesters (even anarchists) were boisterously arguing with Hitchens, calling George W. Bush a warmonger and aggressor in an unjustified war based on rumors that Saddam planned to use his alleged WMDs. Hitchens reminded them Congress had voted in favor of Desert Storm to remove the dictator who had oppressed the Iraqi people for twenty-five years. Saddam had violated UN sanctions, steadily refusing UN inspectors into Iraq's nuclear operations. We had no idea if or when Saddam would produce and deploy a nuclear bomb against America or Israel. He had already demonstrated his lack of humanity when he dropped poison gas on the Kurds, his own people.

The dispute between Hitchens and the younger men got louder, turning into a heated altercation. Guests began to leave as the alcohol-charged atmosphere on the terrace turned aggressive and the situation between the men became uncomfortable.

I told Martin I was leaving and he walked me into the elevator. When we got to the lobby I asked the front desk to call a taxi. Martin kissed me goodbye, then turned to return to the action upstairs. I waited for my cab on the hotel steps, reviewing the long day and night. Once back in my hotel room, I was relieved to get into clean sheets for an eight hour sleep.

The next morning, I called Martin at 11:00 a.m in his room at the W Hotel. He promptly answered the phone and told me what had happened after I left the party. It became apparent that Hitchens and one of the bearded men were about to come to blows as the intensity of tempers escalated and alcoholic consumption increased. Finally, someone called hotel security and Hitch's pugnacious adversaries were escorted out of the hotel. Martin and Hitchens stayed on with the few remaining guests until the open bar closed (or had run out of booze). Martin said Hitch had called him at nine that morning as if nothing had happened the night before—no disputation, no partisan altercation, no near fisticuffs, no hotel security... and no hangover. The Hitch was up and ready to go to his scheduled 10 a.m. panel at the Los Angeles Book Festival on the UCLA campus.

Twenty minutes later a driver picked up Hitchens in the W lobby and drove him a few blocks to UCLA for his first panel discussion of a long day ahead. Martin said his best friend, The Hitch, Christopher, never ceased to amaze him with his wit, enthusiasm, fierce intelligence, and indefatigable *joie de vivre*. At the time, no one—especially Hitchens—could have predicted a few years later the sudden onset of throat cancer would take the life of the great journalist and debater. Christopher Hitchens died eight years later in 2011.

Christopher Hitchens at UCLA party at W Hotel

• • •

When communism failed, it wasn't a good idea that had gone wrong, it was a bad idea that had been sustained with incredible determination in the face of all the commonsense arguments, and at the cost of 20 million lives at least, in Russia, to build the socialist Utopia.

— MARTIN AMIS

Twenty-Six

MARTIN AND LIONEL ASBO: SEATTLE LIBRARY

The last time I saw Martin was in Seattle in October 2012 when he was on a book tour for his recent novel, *Lionel Asbo*. I drove to the (blue) Emerald City to hear his reading at the new Seattle Public Library, which had been funded by Paul Allen, co-founder of Microsoft. Inside the massive auditorium were more than two hundred of Martin's loyal fans.

I went into the large lobby to greet Martin as he arrived surrounded by a cadre of event organizers. A young security man was quick to intercede as I headed towards Martin to shoo me away. When Martin saw the security guard was blocking my approach, he quickly intervened and hugged me, kissing both cheeks, to the consternation of the guard (who was just doing his job.) After our joyful salutations, I asked Martin if we could share a drink after his talk and signing. He told me to meet him at the bar in his Seattle hotel.

Everyone went inside the multi-tiered auditorium that by now was filled to capacity. Martin stepped up to the podium while I took a seat in the second row that I had saved with the book. He read an excerpt from *Lionel Asbo* for his fawning fans, and reminded them he had gone back to the genre he was best known for—bawdy, dark humor; socially polarized characters; upper vs. low-life's; hoodlums that exploited the naïveté and vulnerability of others (for amusement.)

Martin changed the subject to American politics, having just covered the Republican National Convention in Tampa, Florida, for Newsweek magazine (that has since gone online now). His 99 percent Democrat audience greeted his vitriolic report on the G.O.P. candidate for president, Mitt Romney, enthusiastically. When Martin asked who planned to vote for Romney only two hands were raised in the crowded auditorium.

Martin criticized Mitt Romney for his "lack of social connection" to American middle and lower classes, his "disastrous trip" to England and Israel, and for his Mormon religion—even though Mitt's religion was not an issue in the election.

Martin also joked that if VP-nominee, Paul Ryan, had a daughter he should call her Ayn Ryan (pronounced 'Eye-an Ry-an') mocking Ryan's devotion to novelist-philosopher, Ayn Rand. He also amused on Ayn and Ron Rand.

During the talk Martin gave his routine personal anecdotes and analogies of famous living and dead authors whom he frequently quoted.

Martin answered questions during Q and A that his fans had asked hundreds of times during the last four decades of public tours and readings. This replay brought to mind his book of essays, *The War Against the Cliché*.[26]

After an upbeat (Martin's word) hurrah for an Obama Democrat victory in November, Martin walked over to a table to sign books for the long queue that was already trailing with people. I left the library and headed for my car. At first, I drove to the wrong hotel, having heard the name wrong, but the valet told me another hotel downtown began with the letter A. Grateful, I tipped him a ten and drove on.

When I found the Martin's hotel, I parked on a side street, even though I now drive a Benz, I don't like to give my SUV to valets unless there's no other place to park. A nice man walking by gave me more

---

26 Martin Amis. *The War Against the Cliché*. London: Jonathan Cape Ltd; 2001

quarters to fill the two-dollars-an-hour parking meter. I got to the hotel in less than a minute wait in the restaurant. The al fresco terrace tables were occupied, so I went inside and sat at a table in the back corner and ordered a glass of red Zinfandel. Soon Martin arrived, kissed my cheek, and ordered a glass of merlot. We continued to discuss the upcoming presidential election. Martin remained adamant in support for the Democrat candidate, citing disdain for the G.O.P. (Pauline Katz in Philadelphia said she had read Martin refer to "those nasty Republicans." So Martin.)

Martin brought up Mitt Romney's religion again and held it against him as one exceptionally unrealistic. Martin's contention: how can you vote for a someone who believes in a religion founded by a preacher who discovered a Christian bible in the ground of upstate New York in 1830? I conceded his point as a salient epistemological argument; although I reminded him another religion—one followed by billions in the world—was also based on divine revelations spoken to a prophet in a cave in the Arabian Desert.

Martin retorted that Islam began in the 7th Century whereas Joseph Smith founded Mormonism in the 19th Century after he claimed to find the Mormon bible in North America. Martin expounded that people should know better by now than to believe in divine miracles.

Throughout our conversation, a fog of grief shrouded over Martin's shoulders. His friend of forty years, Christopher Hitchens, had died of cancer within the last year. Martin confessed he didn't feel as alive now that The Hitch was no longer around.

Martin had sat at Hitch's bedside during the last few months of chemotherapy, but the cancer metastasized, and Christopher Hitchens finally died in December 2011. Martin had not yet recovered from the death of his best friend; the pain of loss was palatable in his steely eyes.

"You'll see Hitch again." I told him, feeling his pain.

Martin shot me a perturbed look.

I quickly countered, "I don't mean the religious stuff. Seriously, it's quantum mechanics."

Taking this in, he said nothing.

We finished our wine and moved outside to the fresh air sidewalk. The hotel valet took a photo of Martin and me on my cell phone. He told me the last stop of his tour was in Vancouver, BC, and he'd be alone. I repeated what Stanley told Blanch DuBois in *A Streetcar Named Desire* [27] "We've had this date with each other from the beginning." Martin smiled at the scenario, and we kissed each other's cheek au revoir.

Martin and me in Seattle

---

27 Tennessee Williams. *A Streetcar Named Desire* (play, 1947) New York: Signet, 1951

Bibliography

Amazon.com: Books: Martin Amis author page:

https://www.amazon.com/Martin-Amis/e/B000APW594/ref=sr_tc_2_0?qid=1505721997&sr=1-2-ent

Amis, Martin. *The Rachel Papers.* London: Jonathan Cape, Ltd., 1973; New York: Alfred A. Knopf, 1974

Amis, Martin. *Other People: A Mystery Story.* London: Jonathan Cape, Inc., (1981) 208 pages.

Amis, Martin. *Money: A Suicide Note.* New York: Viking Penguin Inc., Mar. 29, 1985

Amis, Martin. *The Moronic Inferno and Other Visits to America.* New York: Viking Adult; (Jan. 1987) 208 pp.

Amis, Martin. *Einstein's Monsters.* London: Jonathan Cape, Ltd., 1987

Amis, Martin. "Insight at Flame Lake." *Vanity Fair* June 1987. p. 98-126+

Amis, Martin. *London Fields.* New York: Harmony Books, 1989

Amis, Martin. "An Exclusive Extract From His New Novel: Seduction in Cold Blood:" *GQ Gentleman's Quarterly: British Edition* August 1989, p.138–224.

Amis, Martin. *Time's Arrow.* New York: Harmony Books, (Oct. 23, 1991)

Amis, Martin "Lolita Reconsidered," *The Atlantic Monthly* Sept. 1992, p. 109-120.

Amis, Martin. *Visiting Mrs. Nabokov and Other Excursions.* London: Jonathan Cape Ltd., (1993) 288 pages.

Amis, Martin. "Straight Fiction," *Esquire* Dec. 1995 (Fiction) p.138-148.

Amis, Martin. *The Information.* American edition: New York: Harmony Books (1995) 374 pages.

Amis, Martin. *Night Train.* London: Jonathan Cape Ltd., 1997. New York: Harmony Books, (1998) 175 pages.

Amis, Martin, *Heavy Water and Other Stories.* New York: Harmony Books (Jan.1999) 208 pages.

Amis, Martin. *Experience: A Memoir;* New York: 1st Vintage International ed. (June 2001) 432 pages.

Amis, Martin. *The War Against Cliché: Essays and Reviews 1971-2000.* London: Jonathan Cape Ltd., 2001; New York, Vintage (July 16, 2002) 528 pages

Amis, Martin. *Koba the Dread: Laughter and the Twenty Million.* New York: Miramax, (July 17, 2002) 320 pp; Vintage (Sept. 9, 2003) 336 pp.

Amis, Martin. *Yellow Dog.* New York: Miramax Books (Hyperion) 2003

Amis, Martin. *House of Meetings.* London: Jonathan Cape Ltd., 2006

Amis, Martin, *The Second Plane: September 11: Terror and Boredom.* New York: Knopf, (April 1, 2008)

Amis, Martin, *Lionel Asbo: State of England.* New York: Alfred A. Knopf, 1st Edition. 2012

Amis, Martin, *Zone of Interest.* New York: Knopf. (Aug. 2014) 306 pp.

Amis, Martin. *The Rub of Time: Bellow, Nabokov, Hitchens, Travolta, Trump: Essays and Reportage, 1986-2016.* New York, Knopf. (Feb. 2017)

Celine, Louis-Ferdinand. *Journey To the End of the Night.* New York: New Directions, 1949; Translated by Ralph Manheim, New York: New Directions Books. 1983

Exley, Frederick. *A Fan's Notes: A Fictional Memoir.* New York: Harper & Row, 1968

Fussell, Paul. *Class: A Guide Through the American Status System.* New York: Simon & Schuster, 1st edition (Oct.1983) 208 pages

—*The Anti-Egoist: Kingsley Amis, Man of Letters.* Oxford University Press 1994

Glazek, Christopher. "The Secretive Family Making Billions From the Opioid Crisis." *Esquire* Nov 2017

Hanford, WA. "Nuclear Waste Clean Up": https://en.wikipedia.org/wiki/Hanford_Site

Heilpern, John. "Our Man in Brooklyn," *Vanity Fair* Sept. 2012 Print https://www.vanityfair.com/culture/2012/09/martin-amis-writing-and-aging

Lahr, John. London Fields: Book review, *Vogue* April 1990, Books: p. 274-278.

Marx, Arthur. *Everybody Loves Somebody Sometimes: (especially himself): The Story of Dean Martin and Jerry Lewis,* New York: Hawthorn Books, 1974

McEwan, Ian. *Amsterdam*. New York: Nan A. Talese/Doubleday, Dec. 1, 1998.

McFarland, Sabrina. Passages: Martin Amis, *People Magazine* Sept 27, 1993. p. 57.

Delgado, Martin and Sandra LaVille. "Martin Attacked in £500,000 'greed row.'" London: *Evening Standard*, Daily Newspaper: Jan 6, 1995. p. 5.   Print

Herbert, Susannah. "Martin Amis goes the way of 'the Jackal.'" London: *The Daily Telegraph*: (*The Telegraph*) Jan. 5, 1995. p. 3.   Print

Richman, Rick. "Bellow, Hitchens, and COMMENTARY." *Commentary Magazine* Nov. 8, 2010, New York, NY.

Shnayerson, Michael. "Famous Amis." *Vanity Fair* May 1995, p.132-162 (Contrib. p.20)

Stanley, Alessandra. "Talk Ends and Spin Begins: Tina Brown Has No Regrets." New York Times http://www.nytimes.com/2002/01/20/us/talkand-spin-begins-tina-brown-has-no-regrets.html-ends-

Tepperman, Jonathan. "Stranger Than Fiction." Newsweek April 14, 2008, p.77

Wallace-Wells, David. "Martin Amis Talks Terrorism, Pornography, Idyllic Brooklyn, and American." New York Magazine July 2012

Williams, Tennessee. *A Streetcar Named Desire* (Broadway play, 1947) New York: Signet, 1951

CPSIA information can be obtained
at www.ICGtesting.com
Printed in the USA
LVHW081803190420
654025LV00015B/2607

9 781542 408721